GET DOWN TO BUSINESS

SHALOM KLEIN

LEADERS IN GLOBAL PUBLISHING

Published by Motivational Press, Inc.
1777 Aurora Road
Melbourne, Florida, 32935
www.MotivationalPress.com

Manufactured in the United States of America.

ISBN: 978-1-62865-585-8

CONTENTS

ACKNOWLEDGEMENTS

I've always wanted to write a book but would have never been able to turn it into a reality without the inspiration and support from the following people:

- to my good friend and business partner Moe Vela was the one who pushed me to take my story and put it in written form

- to Michael Mann who unknowingly set the "Get Down To Business" journey in motion when he first pitched me on the idea of hosting a radio show

- to Ben Dorfman for the invaluable support throughout the process of this book

- to the many people that taught me key values and that I consider my mentors, in particular Brad Alter, Avi Goldfeder, David Jacobson, Michael Lorge, Howard Rieger and Abbie Weisberg

- to my Skokie and Keshet communities that inspire me to keep being involved and giving back

- to my parents and my sister, Moshe & Leah Klein and Miriam Lipnick, who were a part of my story from day #1

- to my brilliant Goldendoodle Buddy who spent time with me on many late night and early morning drafting sessions

- and of course to my life partner Eli who is by far my biggest supporter

MY STORY

SHALOM KLEIN, ENTREPRENEUR, BUSINESSMAN, NETWORKER, LEADER

I AM A BORN LEADER. Not because I was born into privilege, but because ever since I was young I've been one to step up. I've been willing to put the work in.. I was never the best learner in school, but I was always the one to organize the kids and even the teachers around me, driving the organization and management of parades, rallies, and holiday events. I was never the most studious kid, but I was always the most involved kid. That's why, in a way, my trajectory has been plotted since the beginning.

I didn't get much from my early education. I got a structure and a smattering of values (which I was already learning at home), but the quality of my education wasn't top-notch; the ideas that could have inspired me at school lacked the draw to do so. Later on, I did learn from advanced education the best practices that organizations use to be effective. I learned about respecting other people's perspectives. I learned history and how it applies to the evolution of organizational ideas. However, even these educational insights I don't regularly use for business and community; I learn them to teach others. The person that I was in school, the activities I planned, these shaped me more than school (even the schooling of higher education) itself. I learned more outside of school than I ever did while looking at a blackboard.

I got the single most important idea that would propel me on my future path from my father. More than any principle given to me through formal education, this has helped me succeed in business and in life. "If you want something done, do it yourself" was something my dad taught me more than anyone. After his one and only job selling Prudential life insurance in the seventies and eighties, he started his own business and never looked back. He i so entrenched in this idea that it's funny to watch him now, slipping into retirement mode, slowly letting others take on his projects. Though he can't really hand everything off; he's starting new things even now. Since growing up with him, I've written my own playbook and helped others write their own, but this foundational idea has continually shaped my approach to how I live daily.

Everybody goes through a journey. There are roadblocks, speed bumps, andunexpected curves. My story is like yours; it's far from straightforward. After growing up with in a hard-working family and learning from my father, then getting whatever I could out of elementary and high school, I planned on becoming a rabbi. I loved (and still love) community work, so I figured that was a balanced, established place to start. I thought that I could bring people together behind the pulpit, inspiring them to work on charitable initiatives together. I went so far as to attend religious colleges in Detroit and Israel because I believed being a rabbi was the best path for me.

After coming back from Israel, I took a step back and reexamined my course. I realized what I really wanted was to do influential community work,which I could do that without being a rabbi. I could do that just by focusing on that work by its own merits.

I went back to the person who had first inspired me and joined my Dad in business at the family accounting firm, working with him in marketing, sales, and organizational operations. I developed a strategy for time management, giving me the hours to become more involved in community work even as I furthered my career. I developed a desire to help others even more than when I was on the path to become a rabbi and started Jewish Business to Business Networking, which was one of the most influential jobs and business networking organizations in the Chicagoland area.

I pushed myself to become even more communally involved and people started noticing. They handed me business opportunities, opportunities to take leadership roles in communal organizations, and consulting opportunities. I took many of the opportunities given to me, but specifically, the consulting opportunities I used to build up a consulting practice. I started working with dozens of businesses and nonprofits, helping them with external affairs issues, marketing, public relations, and many other areas that I'd developed expertise with just through my involvement in business and community. I started traveling all over the world to consult with companies wherever they needed me.

Luckily, taking on my role as a consultant didn't shift my focus — it allowed me to stay involved in community as much as I want to. Now I spend more than fifty percent of my time each day involved with community projects that don't make me money—they cost me money! I'm okay with that; I want to give back as much as I can while living my life as best as I can.

Now, all of my roles have expanded. I am the chair of more boards in more communities than ever, I still volunteer at one-off events, and I travel more places as a consultant than I ever did. I'm also doing things that I never would have expected and don't necessarily have a direct connection to business or community: I'm finishing my doctorate and I'm writing this book. And I'm happy; not every day, but most days. I'm happy that I've become involved, that my life is filled with meaningful activities, that I'm always helping people.

The story is still being written. I don't think that in five years from now I'll be doing the same things that I'm doing today. But I'll be getting things done the same way and that what's most important. The practices that have led to my success so far are will continue to lead me to my success. I'll always be able to use them to work toward good causes and to work with good companies. o matter who I'm working with, I do it in my way: there is only one Shalom Klein.

I don't want anyone to look at my story and say, "He just did what he set out to do andsome unexpected events happened along the way, but everything worked out as planned." Nothing worked out exactly as planned; nothing came easy. It wasn't easy making the choice not to become a rabbi; I doubted myself and had to overcome that doubt. It wasn't easy getting involved in community organizations and branching out from the family accounting firm to get into consulting. I've had issues with family, health, business, inspiration, and spirituality. Every issue that one can have along the path: I've had it. I'm a very imperfect person; I've tried hard to be successful, but I've still screwed up many times along the way.

But that's the way it should be. You try things that work, you try things that don't work, and you find your footing:you find your ground. Those occasional setbacks don't mean that your life isn't moving ahead. You need to screw up a little bit in life because there's no playbook—you have to learn by trial and error. I've found that though my life hasn't been easy or the path clear, and though my decisions haven't lead me to the place that I originally planned, I'm in the place that's right for me. Most people who lead balanced lives can relate to this sentiment.

Here's the real difference between my story and most people's: I work harder. I get up earlier than most people are willing to get up and I work later than most people are willing to work. I travel farther, go to more meetings, take on more obligations. I don't question whether or not I can do it—working hard is who I am. It's more effort, but it's brought me farther.

Here's something else: I focus more on relationships. I take one-on-one meetings no matter the person; I make time for the people I meet and I am always meeting new people. I know how to leverage relationships. Through building relationships, I've met some of the best people in the world and they've helped me to do what I love.

I feel fortunate that I was able to discover these two life secrets early on because I know that some people live out their entire lives without finding these secrets at all. Many more people know about these ideas in principle, but fail to utilize them in their lives. I feel fortunate that I found that I wanted to balance business and community early on. These things have been consistent motivational pillars in my life; some people have no pillars to support them. I can be as involved as I want to be with them; I can reap as much benefit from them as I'd like—and that freedom to be involved is also something that many people never experience.

Many people brush off communal involvement as something they can do when they retire; they look only to money for fulfillment. I'm lucky enough to say that I don't want to be the wealthiest person in the worldI want to be comfortable. I don't want to avoid monetary obligations and run away to Paraguay, but I want to stay devoted to community and to those things that give me strength outside of a paycheck. I value both and because I put in the hard work and build those relationships, that value comes back to me.

My story is like many peoples but it's also different. Like so many others I went on a journey with a winding path. But I ended up in a radically different place than most people because I consistently show the willingness to push beyond what others are willing to do.

Others should have taken the lead on the issues that I'm involved in—there should have already been a small business networking organization in the Jewish community; why the hell was it me that had to do it? But that's just it—there were causes that I wanted to be represented that just weren't there. It is natural for anyone when they move to a new city and they want to become involved with organizations or causes to join. But what happens if there is nothing? That's what I experienced. I didn't get pushback; I found an empty playing field. Clearly there are other people who could have started JB2B but I was the only person who recognized that lack and wanted to do something about it. So that's what I did—I started on an organization that looked like the one I wanted to exist.

The same process happened with the Skokie Economic Development Commission. I didn't see anything like the commission out there, a structure for the small business community to be involved in Skokie, so I stepped up to build that structure. The same process happened with my radio-show; I saw that people needed regular advice on business, entrepreneurship, and networking so I gave it to them. Even with JCC WRP, though there had been an organization doing the same thing decades ago. I revived it and made it operate in a way that's effective and completely new—it won't go defunct like its predecessor because I've made it into a wholly different entity.

I started these initiatives because I wanted to; I became involved in the things I do because I felt the drive. I didn't inherit any of this from anyone else; I started it all myself. When there is an infrastructure in place, I'm perfectly happy to use it as I did with Keshet, the Jewish special needs organization that's been around for thirty years and will be around for longer than the next thirty years. I took a seat on the young leadership board, then I chaired the young leadership board, I was on the board of directors and now I chair the board of directors. But by and large that hasn't been the norm.

Maybe I'm not the person that should have done any of this. I'm not the perfect messenger; I wasn't then and I'm not now. I don't have a formal background in job counseling or business—I never set out to be a networking guru. Still, I did get that radio show. Who am I to have a radio-show? I should be listening to other radio-shows, not advising people with my own. But because I see the need, I become the right person to start these initiatives, and the right person to advise others on how to do so.

I write this book partly out of self interest. I'm hoping that people will read this book, take in my story, learn my lessons, and become inspired to follow after me into a path of greater involvement in business and community. I want to see these people at the meetings I go to, volunteer with me at events, advocate with me on issues that we both care about. I don't tell my story and I don't give you what I've learned on my journey so that these ideas can remain pretty words on a page. My hope is that the more people that read my book, the more impact communities and small businesses will feel from the people that really want to implement my lessons and my truths.

The title of this book is Get Down to Business. A just-as-good title: Roll Up Your Sleeves and Do It. Anybody can do any of the things that I did. Anybody can work hard; anybody can build relationships. It doesn't matter who you are, where you grew up, what your past educational or family experience has been like. You don't need to be a born leader. You can be making significant changes to your lifestyle and your habits; you can be coming back from challenges that are even harder than I've faced.

You can get ideas out of this book to change your life for the better. But you have to make this book truly your own. Make the titles of the chapters to anything that will fit your own life. Make "Small Business" into "My Printing Shop", Religion into "My Church", Community into "My SPCA Involvement"—whatever you like. They can act as the signposts to a more involved, more complete life. But don't simply talk about it; just roll up your sleeves and do it. As given by Benjamin Franklin: "Well done is better than well said." Work hard, develop ideas, meet people, pay it forward, leverage every opportunity, make it happen. Read this book, not to become me, but to become the real you—the one that wants to get involved, the one that wants contribute to their community, be better at their job, and do the work that needs to be done. I'm Shalom Klein and I'm going to show you how to get down to business.

TIME MANAGEMENT

Plan it, Say it, Do it

CHANCES ARE GOOD THAT AT some point in your life, you are going to spend a lot of your time tackling time management. You'll read about it in books, take an in-person or online class, or teach yourself using an (expensive) electronic or paper day planner to organize, prioritize, and schedule your day. At the end of your efforts, I'm guessing you'll say the same thing as when you started: I feel like I can't get everything done. My answer—everything you've ever learned about managing time is a waste of time because it isn't working.

Before you can even begin to manage time, you need to learn the real nature of time. The Mirriam-Webster dictionary defines time as "the point or period when something occurs" . It is simply when events happen on our agreed-upon timeline.

Our own understanding of time jives with that definition intuitively, but time itself doesn't necessarily operate on those rigid terms. Many people have thought about time differently as you will learn to do.

Multiple systems of time telling predate our Westernized Gregorian Solar calendar and some continue to exist alongside ours. Judaism and Islam adhere to the Lunar calendar, marking time by the cycle of the Moon; Buddhism uses a combined Lunisolar calendar to keep time using both the Sun and Moon. Judaism and Islam still set the timing of their holidays by this calendar, even though doing so shifts the date of these holidays year to year on the universal calendar.

To many indigenous peoples, time itself is foreign. The Piraha Tribe of the Amazons have no concept of time—their lives are completely lived in the present—whereas the Hopi Native American Tribe only mark time with two words in their vocabulary: sooner and later.

For Nomadic tribes today, as with Fertile Crescent peoples in the dawn of civilization, the seasons define both space and time—they determine where and when nomads will travel.

Countries move at different paces. The United States and Japan rank as some of the fastest moving countries while Greece and other Mediterranean countries rank slowest. Related to this is the convention of the nine-to-five workday, with two week vacations and weekends off. All these taken-for-granted American office norms are very recent phenomena, only within the last hundred or so years, and you'll see how quickly they fall away if you are building a new business.

Point being? All time is relative. Time shifts by location, culture, religion, even era. Most relevant to time management, however, is personal perception of time—a flexible, fickle factor helping to explain why people experience time differently.

Time flies or drags depending on what you're doing. Two hours at the Department of Motor Vehicles can feel like twelve years, whereas time spent jamming out at your favorite concert feels like twelve seconds. The reason: your perception of time relates to how much you pay attention to time. The more bored you are looking at the people in line ahead of you at the DMV, the more you will focus on the time and attempt to anticipate the next moment. The more engaged you are with the activity, the less you will look at the clock and the more time will fly. A watched pot never boils, a watched clock never ticks.

Luckily, the opposite holds true for memories, a process called the holiday paradox. That concert will give you music for hours when you later think of it in your head, but the DMV will barely register for two agonizing seconds. The brain encodes our exciting new experiences while passing over the same tired ones. This also explains why time appears to pass more quickly as we age—we fill our young lives with countless new learning experiences, slowing time and encoding memory, but as we get older we tend to limit these experiences.

The traditional time management advice flattens and minimizes the mutable aspect of time, not allowing you to view time as flexible. Rather, it encourages you to place your activities on your personal timeline as if they were just random numbered objects on a physical line in space.

Instead, get a grasp over time quality before you understand time quantity. Understand the difference between how time operates for you and your activities VS how it operates independently.

A clock times traditional, measured time, otherwise known as clock-time. Your internal clock flows with an ever-changing speed; it times your own real-time. The real reason time management gadgets and systems don't work isn't because you are using them wrong. Those systems are designed to manage clock-time. Clock-time will be less relevant to you reaching your goals than real-time. Getting control of your real-time may seem daunting. After all, people don't seem to have a choice about the way their minds respond to activities.

But I've already hinted that this assumption is false: real-time is a controllable mental space. Using the holiday paradox, if time spent during youth felt long because we were filling it with fresh and exciting activities, we can slow time down by keeping our lives stocked with new activities even as we age. On a day to day level, using the opposite side of the holiday paradox—looking at VS not looking at the watch—we should do the things we most enjoy when we will most enjoy them. In a work context, we should schedule the most productive things when we will be the most productive. We should maximize our productivity and our enjoyment of everything we do. Then we will be able to do more, produce more, and enjoy what we do more as we actually do it! Our real-time will govern our clock-time because we'll never be looking at the clock.

Basically what that means is this: you have more control over time than you realize. Control time and concentrate on the most important things first, nurture better relationships, and remove self-sabotage or self-limitation.

Shift the focus from time slots to the activities you fill your schedule with to give real-time the presence it deserves, mirroring the prominence it actually takes in your life VS clock-time. This removes stress by training your mind to focus on 'what' rather than 'when'—freeing your mind (partially) from laboring excessively over scheduling details.

There are only three ways to spend time: thoughts, conversations, or action; or more pragmatically: plan, say, do. Regardless of the type of business you own, your work does and will continue to comprise these three items. Understanding when and how each category will function best for you is one of the keys to getting control over your time.

You might say, "Thinking? Planning? I'm doing that all day long!" Similarly, "You don't think I already have meetings?" And lastly, "You can't possibly be telling me that I'm not already doing things, take a look at how much I've been running around for months, for years!"

Believe me, I know, and I'm sure all these things are true. But the first question you have to ask yourself is: "what am I really doing?" Chances are, much of the thinking, conversations, and action you spend time on throughout out the day isn't actually building your business—it's just wasting your time. Even though you consider yourself productive, you are really just taxing yourself with unnecessary burdens. You can bet this

----

is going to affect your enjoyment of what you are doing long-term and ultimately sabotage your sense of real-time completely.

Before you know when to do, you have to know what to do, and what not to do. So what are you actually doing? Find out. Carry around a schedule with space for notes and record all your thoughts, conversations, and activities for one week marking down time spent on each and rating on a ten-point scale the estimated effectiveness of every block of time spent on each category. For thoughts, also focus on times throughout the day that you daydreamed, thought about random things in line at the DMV, and of course, thought about business while at the office. For conversations, include talking to family and friends as well as business meetings. For activities, not just making key business moves, but also watching online cat videos.

This exercise may sound labor intensive, but this will help you understand how much real work you get done during the day and where your other precious moments are going. You'll find out how much time is spent producing results and how much time is wasted on unproductive thoughts, conversations, and actions. In this way, you will move from thoughts, conversations, and action to plan, say, do.

This doesn't mean that you need to give up all your free time. Spend at least fifty percent of your time engaged in thoughts, conversations, and actions that produce most of the desired results for your business. Even the other fifty percent of the time shouldn't just be free-form—it's scheduled leisure time; your appointments for yourself. Bifurcating your time will allow you to enjoy each rather than running back and forth inside your own head (part of flow, which I'll explain later in this chapter). You won't waste even your free time anymore—you will value it.

Instead of assigning a general to-do list that gets longer and longer to the point where your life is filled with unworkable tasks center your commitments around plan, say, do. Focus on designating blocks of time that are only used for each of these activities and schedule when they will begin and end with discipline.

If you plan something, set aside a half an hour to an hour to constructively think about the project, using brainstorming, outlines, timelines—whatever you need to zoom in on that project and free yourself from distraction.

If you are having a conversation, set aside a realistic amount of time for the call. Make sure that you aren't under pressure to be curt and curtail your conversational goals. Set those goals: take the first thirty minutes before every call and decide what results you want. Know what success looks like before you start and you will actually reach for that success during the call.

If you engage in an activity, draw on the work you prepared during your scheduled planning block and ideas that came up in relevant conversations. Aim to get personal tasks done quickly and efficiently; it can be easier to count the minutes when you aren't with someone else.

Take time after each designated plan, say, or do period and determine whether your desired result was achieved and if not, what was missing. If you can't integrate those missing pieces into your next block of plan, say or do, don't let the ruminations bleed all over your schedule. Allow them to rest in your next activity period.

Conversations are a two-way street—you have to be present to enjoy them and to get your mutual goals accomplished. Genuine natural dialogue is a requirement of good conversation in business just as in your personal life. Disconnect all instant messaging; give people in front of you your full attention. Schedule a time to answer emails and return phone calls rather than concentrating on them when you don't need to.

For that matter, in all plan say or do, a solid rule of thumb is to shut down needless computer-generated distraction during your working blocks. Forget social use of FaceBook and other forms of social media during the work day. Let's use these tools to just generate business!

This isn't just a tirade against multitasking or social indulgence. When talking real-time, activities intersect with the scientific concept called flow. Flow means to be completely engrossed in an activity so that time ceases to exist. When studied in a lab, top musicians and athletes display the same neural networks firing when they are in the state of flow; their passion can be measured in their brain. Mathematicians in flow can work at problems for ten hours, not getting up to use the bathroom, eat, or drink Part of the reason why those athletes and musicians get into flow so easily is because after putting in those years of practice, their performance is their passion. Flow relates to happiness; in fact, some postulate that flow provides the very essence of happiness itself through the feeling of perfect fulfillment.

Your goal is to get as close to the state of flow in your business and personal activities as possible so that clock-time disappears and you can be fully rooted in real-time. Scheduling both your free and business time positively affects your overall state of flow. More designated, uninterrupted time increases the likelihood of achieving flow when with family or friends as it does with colleagues or business activities.

Because you will get into flow more easily the more you enjoy your work, it's incumbent on you get out there and find a job you like. When you flow, looking at the clock will be the furthest thing from your mind, even if you find the task difficult, as long as you find it rewarding.

Nevertheless, it may be that in the short-term, you're working a less than ideal position. Keep this from affecting your real-time. Don't look at the clock more than needed to make your appointments. If the clock on the computer screen draws your eyes, put a piece of paper over it to discipline yourself.

Setting specific times for actions and removing distractions hugely assists getting into flow. But, especially if you are an entrepreneur, you will frequently be interrupted and pulled in different directions every single day you are building your business. This is a serious disruption in flow. Luckily, you don't need to answer the phone just because it's ringing or to respond to an e-mail just because it showed up on your computer screen. While you cannot eliminate interruptions, filter out all but the most essential and decide how much time you need to spend on them as they come up.

Minimize these interruptions by scheduling time to confer with the people who might otherwise interrupt you. Make time to pull away from what you're doing. Office hours are just another way of saying planned interruptions. Eventually you'll have a better sense of what demands immediate attention now and what can be deferred to uninterrupted interruption time.

Don't be afraid to assert timely boundaries with others around you. Put a "do not disturb" sign on your door when you absolutely must get work done. It won't cause people to think you are a moody teen—it will enhance your reputation as a diligent associate.

Scheduling conversations properly means being flexible with your schedule to accommodate your business partners. Trading endless emails creates an aggravating virtual hamster wheel, so be the first to compromise on the time whenever you can. Setting up a good time to meet quickly relieves initial pressure and proves your togetherness.

Sometimes, unavoidably, you'll be faced with a balancing act where the only times to meet simply won't work for you. Perhaps the other person utilizes a radically different communication or scheduling style from you, or circumstances beyond your control prevent you from connecting. Don't set yourself up for a conversational fiasco by taking a time that will bend you over backwards. Don't take a 5AMmeeting if you're not a morning person! Don't take a business meeting during your daughter's wedding! Instead, respectfully ask if some of the other people you plan to meet during the week would agree to move their meetings. You don't need to make the reasons explicit to the people you are rescheduling, so don't be afraid to use this method to balance out your own schedule. People understand that schedules change.

Worst case scenario: it's better to take a breath and realize that it just might not be the right time to meet with this partner. Conditions could change and you may still be able meet later. You never want to be late or not show up. Show up. Always.

An overarching theme with planning activities: only do things when you can really accomplish them. This is even more important than doing things only when you will enjoy them. You'll reach certain failure if you try to do something when it can't be done. Today may not be the right time to start or manage certain aspects of your business. That's okay. Just as with scheduling conversations, the best move is to optimize your enjoyment through realistic productivity. If you try to force an activity to happen, you'll destroy your enjoyment with unnecessary pressure before you give up on a project that might have met success if you'd had the patience to start later.

Realize that it is impossible to get everything done right now, but that many things can be done in stages with proper prioritization. If you prioritize the most time-appropriate projects first you'll move more quickly through them with the confidence that they can be done now. You'll prepare yourself for the more difficult projects approaching you in the future without even thinking about it. You'll flow and you'll be in tune with real-time.

As you progress in your ability to time-manage and begin to prioritize and assign time by activity, you'll see a gradual increase in the amount that you are able to do and a decrease in the amount that you will need to reschedule or restructure your time. As your capacity and your passion for your activities grow, you'll be able to be flexible in ways you never thought possible.

Busy people only get busier. You'll fit more work on your schedule as you take on more obligations because obligations, paradoxically, keep you more accountable and therefore, more on time with your time management. Believe me, if you don't schedule your time, something will fill it for you. Then you'll be busy with the non-essential and as your ability to fulfill your existing obligations plummets your lack of productivity will skyrocket.

I'm a busy person. I don't sleep much and I drink more coffee than I do water. Yet no matter how jam-packed my own schedule gets, people still feel that my schedule is always open for them. My capacity to build a schedule bends to my passion and my life in real-time—my passion and my life don't bend to the rigid 24-hrs that so much time management advice holds sacrosanct.

Don't get me wrong, I still have a calendar. As I've said before, everything is on my calendar; even the time I put aside for myself. And I'm still clear when an appointment won't work for me. But I've been doing this so long that I've built up a lot of good faith with the people I work with. I embolden them to be up front with me because I am always up front with them. I also keep good on appointments with myself just as I would any other person. After all, how can you show up for others if you aren't even there for yourself?

Before we go forward, I'll let you in on a humbling secret. The odds are good that twenty percent of your thought conversations and activities will produce eighty percent of results. Twenty percent! Looks like nothing, and this is a major cause of the reason that even when you manage your time perfectly, you can still feel as if you're running around in circles. But you won't ever know where this twenty percent will fall in your entire plan, say, do. You'll be moving through your day and discover a gem in your work that you've been hunting for months. As you bring more focus to your activities, you'll notice these milestones more.

More importantly, every time you stick to your commitments, you become a stronger business partner and a stronger entrepreneur. Even if the activity doesn't result in something long-term, you've still used that time to build your control over time, to build your passion, to build your relationships, and to become a more reliable person.

I've been called "the busiest man in the world." But people say over and over again that I commit 100% to every project I work on. They say already I've done more than people twice my age. They say I get things done. Congresswoman Jan Schakowsky said I was a "force of nature" and that "everything he does is successful." It may seem ludicrous that I can do so much for so many others, fitting all these commitments into my day and giving everything I have to each project.

A few years back, I donated my bone marrow to save a complete stranger. The appointment went through its own rescheduling process; there was a moment when I thought I wouldn't be able to help this person—that we might have been too late. In the end, thank God, we did get the appointment scheduled. It was *incredibly* important that I show up. Here's what the doctor said about the process:

"By the time (Shalom) is getting the injections," Dr. Leonard Klein said, "the recipient has already gone through a round of usually heavy doses of chemotherapy. So if (Shalom) doesn't show up here on time, and there's a delay or he decides not to do it, ...the patient could be in trouble."

In that case, for that person, my showing up meant the difference between life and death. All of my time management preparation came under test at that moment. I passed not because I'd spent years harrying myself and putting pressure on others about timing details, but because I learned to prioritize my passions every day, to plan, say and do—to show up for others and for myself. Plan it, say it, do it, and you will feel it: feel your own presence with everything thing you do, feel others recognizing you as present for them, and feel yourself existing in present time.

LOCAL NEIGHBORHOOD

BE WHERE YOU ARE, LIVE WHO YOU ARE

THE STORY OF YOUR NEIGHBORHOOD— where you live, where you talk with your neighbors, where you greet people as you walk your dog— that story will inform how successful you are at building relationships and strengthening your community. The more you give to your neighborhood, the more the place where you live will thrive and the easier your day-to-day life will become. You can't expect to get along with your neighbors all the time, but the more you support the foundations of your neighborhood, the more your neighbors will respect you and the more you'll have to talk about with them!

I envision a world where businesses are thriving, people have jobs, infrastructure is up-to-date, and public institutions are healthy and expanding their services to those who need it most. But this vision, a vision of prosperous large communities, can't be achieved without the concerted efforts of people within individual neighborhoods working with each other and without sister neighborhoods partnering together. We as citizens of our neighborhoods need to learn from one another so that we can achieve more on a national and global scale.

When I walk around my neighborhood, I let my guard down. I walk into my favorite Starbucks with my workout clothes on; I don't feel that I need to portray a stiff business persona in the place that I live. If I took you around my neighborhood, this is what I'd say: this Starbucks is my Starbucks, that grocery store is my grocery store, that chocolate shop is my chocolate shop. I connect with the places I frequent; they become part of my lifestyle and more importantly, part of my life. Even the streets themselves, the parks that I sit down in, the benches on the street I pass by, the trees overhead—they are part of my beloved corner that I live in. People will ask, what do you do? My answer will be my business orientation, but it won't be who I am or where I come from. I travel all over the world for my job, but my neighborhood, block for block, feels like my home.

The people that you live by in your neighborhood, though they may come from different particular communities, can be as much a part of your neighborhood home as your neighborhood places. In the random scheme of things, you might never meet your neighbors; running in completely separate cohorts, holding different values, being different ages: all things that in a different world would keep you from ever meeting.

Luckily, the fact that you live by them allows you to share common ground and become friends, touching their identity, even with little else shared between you. This luck can even happen transhistorically, as in West Rogers Park, one of my neighborhoods. In the 1960's when my father walked Devon Avenue all the way down to Sheridan Avenue, there were only Jewish institutions. Now Asian, Croatian, Hispanic, Assyrian, African-American along with Jewish people call West Rogers Park Home. In a neighborhood that was once a uniform community,now many people add their uniqueness, their culture, their lifestyle to the experience that all neighbors can share. Neighborhoods break randomness into something whole and cohesive. They tear down barriers and lay the groundwork for trust.

While this trust is planted between neighbors by happenstance, it grows into sustained commonality. Then you'll feel perfectly comfortable around your neighbors, just as you feel at any space in your neighborhood. If there were a snow day, your kids would be having a snowball fight with all the kids up and down the block. If your car was buried in a mountain of snow, your neighbors would dig you out as you chat with them about local politics. An ideal situation, but one that you can, and must, put within your grasp.

The most beautiful situation occurs when you've invested so much in your community that people know you both on the block where you live and the places you go. Your places and your people intersect. When I walk into Starbucks at 7AM, my time, I'll see people that I know as they walk through the door and all the baristas and managers know my name. This same thing happens at my grocery store and my chocolate shop. I know the places, I know the people, and I know the people within our places.

My own journey to become involved with my neighborhood happened without my thinking about it. I moved to Skokie at a young age; I've grown up here and I shared a life with my close family here. Long before I matured and bought a house in Skokie, laying the groundwork for long-term stability, and continuing the permanence of my life here, I knew I would be involved in the community. My heritage in the neighborhood always meant that I would own a real piece of the land, but my participation wasn't begun through that ownership. As soon as I could after finishing school I joined the Skokie Caucus Party, a political non-partisan mobilization party in Skokie, and, through the process that I will describe later on, I now merit a place on the board.

Aside for political events, we put on a yearly holiday toy drive and raise money for the local food pantry. Organizing and, more importantly, volunteering in these altruistic activities led me to meet my wife. When we married, we strengthened both our connection to each other and and commitment to our neighborhood because we had formed a meaningful relationship around something we cared about and continue to care about. Soon, my increased involvement in the neighborhood had gone on for so long I couldn't imagine it otherwise.

I have a philosophy of neighborhood work. I call it:"don't complain, change." As the Chair of the Skokie Economic Development Council in Skokie I regularly meet with the mayor so we can discuss the future of the neighborhood. When I work with the mayor or other neighborhood officials that shape the future of the neighborhood, I make my voice heard so that the neighborhood will become the way I think it should become. What rights do I or does anyone else have, to complain about something that I could have changed if I had tried?

That's just what was at stake when I went to fight for businesses in Skokie. I got a call from my friend: "Shalom did you hear about this new legislation?" I hadn't.

For me, economics and the way that local businesses thrived was the most important cause to lend my energy when I began work within my neighborhood. I saw the loss of businesses on Dempster and attributed some of that to struggles that small retailers have in general competing with big-box stores and online retailers—both corporate entities that can afford the best advertising.

Neighborhood stores on the other hand, provide a level of convenience that can't be matched by these other services. When a neighborhood like West Rogers Park or a business district like Dempster Street begins to amass block after block of empty storefronts, the life of the neighborhood begins to fade and the lives of neighbors become more difficult, even though they can still use online services and big box stores. I saw businesses in my neighborhood undergoing this struggle. I wanted a healthy balance for the people who ran local shops and their customers, so I when I had the hint that this local legislation might negatively impact the amount that small businesses could advertise to local customers, I went to work.

For local businesses, there are a couple main types of advertising. There's the big above-the-door signs, and other signs on the business itself. There are billboards, and sidewalk advertisements—all crucial to the survival of any given business. This legislation severely limited sidewalk advertisements near parking lots. In particular, it would hurt my own neighborhood business district.

Outrageous! "Have they moved ahead with it?" I asked. "It can be appealed."

I got out on social media and sent the word around to local businesses. Though the Skokie City Council supposedly had asked local businesses for their input, few had actually heard of the ordinance.

Finally I raised such an uproar that Skokie City Council came back to me. "Shalom, we hear you, what can we do to make this go away?" It took even more finagling, but we got the law changed. More importantly, the Skokie government set up a system of advisory councils so that people in the neighborhood could get their voice heard on more issues. Dempster Street Merchants Association arose out of this conflict.

Many Skokie businesses could have had their futures washed away by that legislation. My own stake in my neighborhood and my own stake in my neighborhood's future prompted me to act and make that future better for me and for every part of Skokie.

Skokie is just one of the neighborhoods I now call my own. In 2013, Howard Reiger, the president and CEO of Jewish Federations of North America, called me up. I'd already heard his name many times, read about him and seen pictures of him meeting presidents and other heads-of-state. He knew we had friends in common and he'd heard of the work that I'd been doing in Skokie and wanted to meet me—to get to know me. Revitalization of West Rogers Park was his project in retirement and he looked to draw on my expertise. At that moment, as always, I had many projects going on. After helping them form a new board for revitalization, they looked to hire a consultant from the outside, inevitably coming back to me. Finally, after saying no repeatedly, I remembered my family in West Rogers Park and the connection I share to them and to their neighborhood as well as to Skokie. I said yes.

Since I've become Executive Director of the Jewish Community Council of West Rogers Park (JCCWRP) I've seen some very positive years of growth. JCCWRP exemplifies revival in a way that could be inspiring to you in your own efforts to improve your neighborhood.

Originally founded in 1975, it took over thirty years for the council to become active again in 2012. We made revival a committed part of our agenda, taking a space that gathered dust as an empty lot for twelve years and making it a neighborhood park in 2017. Our biggest push for revival comes for our local library. We're partnering with Albany Park to see how they revived their library and learning how to advocate and renovate ours. We've seen success in our advocacy efforts for businesses, synagogues, organizations and residents in West Rogers Park.

In building the life of West Rogers Park with my own organization, I remember that volunteers keep the enterprise alive. The lifeblood of JCCWRP is the volunteers who, together with the Jewish United Fund Metropolitan of Chicago (JUF) support our work financially and programmatically. They serve our boards and committees, give us direction, and enhances our voice to our elected and appointed officials. We have exciting new initiatives that benefit our community.

An article in the News Star Newspaper reported on the recent progress for the community-wide efforts to secure a new Northtown Branch Library for West Rogers Park. LEARN coalition, of which JCCWRP is a founding member, garnered more than 2,000 signatures with a petition drive urging the city to set the gears in motion. Ald. Debra Silverstein and her husband Sen. Ira Silverstein, the petition's top two signers, state,

"I believe community activism is a powerful tool. I strongly encourage everyone to keep advocating for our neighborhood and our library." In the end we got our library.

Why should you get involved in your neighborhood? Your quality of life will improve as you improve the space in which you move. The people closest to you can become your best connections, in business, in getting a job, in building friendships, relationships and your health. By living in your neighborhood, you take on the responsibility to help the world and people most close to you. Trust me, if you get involved in your neighborhood you will be grateful to yourself for many years to come.

When you decide to personally join the fight to improve your neighborhood, first determine the focus of your involvement. Imagine becoming involved in several specific neighborhood organizations and gauge your feelings about being involved in each. Pursue only those organizations that most interest you so that you will find true motivation in your involvement. For example, if you take an interest in animals, join the Humane Society. If you believe in healing people, volunteer for Red Cross or United Hatzalah. If you care about businesses like I do, become involved with Chamber of Commerce.

Next, volunteer in those organizations. Arlie Russell Hochschild, Professor Emeritus at University of California Berkeley and a premier sociologist studying the emotions that underlay the formation of communal groups writes:

"People who volunteer at the recycling center or soup kitchen through a church or neighborhood group can come to feel part of something 'larger'. Such a sense of belonging calls on a different part of the self than the market calls on. The market calls on our sense of self interest. It focuses on what we get [not give]."

Volunteering channels the general good-will of the neighborhood into focused action that effects positive change. Though you may initially aspire to paid positions in the neighborhoods or to be on the board of the directors, defer these aspirations until after volunteering. While paid positions motivate tremendously in most people's day-to-day life, volunteer positions prove the outstanding worth of someone who feels committed to building a neighborhood independent of career goals.

Think about it—who do you want to help businesses in your neighborhood, someone who will help those businesses that keep him on retainer or someone who will help all businesses in the neighborhood regardless? It's the difference between a neighborhood and a nepotistic pyramid (taken to an extreme).

The same applies to prestige: the ones who will want it are the ones who shouldn't have it. They don't want the work, they want the acclaim, so they'll try not to do the work and get the acclaim anyway.

Be the person to volunteer, to start actualizing your interest in neighborhood organizations through commitment and by participating in a system that rewards honest effort and connects virtuous people. Believe me, your offer to volunteer will be scooped up; neighborhood organizations always need volunteers. You'll start being of service and you'll show others in your neighborhood that this is your cause.

When you've been in your volunteer role for some time, you'll start to hear about opportunities for you or the people close to you; your placement in your neighborhood organization has then made you a connector. Start bringing opportunities these opportunities to your people , and you'll begin to be the leader that others look to in your organizations. You'll draw on the connections you've made, opportunities capitalized on, and start to spearhead new initiatives and build projects out of those seeds. People will follow you into these new ventures, and they'll trust you to be someone that makes the major decisions at your organization..

That's the intelligent, proven method of making it on to the board of directors.

Remember how I said that the volunteer system ensures that people enter organizations for the right reasons? Even so, some people slip past, and it is these self-seekers who will act as hurdles in your ability to build initiatives and become a neighborhood leader. Everyone takes some personal interest in a cause, but for these people, the cause exists for their personal interest. When you or someone like you challenges their desire to operate the cause for themselves, they will start to push and cause problems for the entire organization. Push back, but more importantly, mobilize your base.

Howard Rieger, the same mentor who got me involved in West Rogers Park, once said with regards to neighborhood transformation, "Success will require the commitment of many people." In order to help people help you to overcome the hurdles put in place by self-seekers you have to get them to reach back to their own original commitment, to remember the values that brought them to volunteering initially, and see that what you are doing honors those values. Leaders are only leaders if they have followers. Followers will recognize you as someone who is not a self seeker if you recognize each of them as the early volunteer that you were, with the same truthful desire to help the organization. Moreover, they will believe in you if you can reignite their original desire, and will see that that is not the mode of the self-seekers.

When you've reached those places you yearned for in the beginning, a position on the board of directors, a consultancy, you'll be able to mark your achievement, not just in your title, but in the concrete milestones you've reached. For instance, maybe there was a problem in your neighborhood that everyone ran away from: kids stealing stop signs, unfriendly competition between two businesses, local wildlife run amok—something sticky and hard to unwind. You remember that problem, you saw it when you came in, and said I'm going to fix it. You joined the neighborhood Youth Council and realized that the only way to stop kids from stealing stop signs was to improve and expand after-school care programs. A chain store and a mom-and-pop pharmacy were competing for customers and getting into ad wars in the local paper; you discovered the retail branch's behavior violated the parent company's policy for that chain. There were too many bears in the neighborhood so you worked out a better neighborhood bear sighting protocol with the County Department of Wildlife.

Hillel the Wise, one of the most famous and well-respected sages in ancient Israel, has a saying that religious Jews read on Sabbath afternoons "In place where there are no leaders, be a leader."

All of these problems felt so intractable, so messy, that no one in your neighborhood would touch them. But when you look back and you realize that you are the person that stepped up and took on the problem, you'll see that that is the reason you deserve your leadership position. If no one steps up to become a leader, then there are no leaders, and problems never get fixed. Neighborhoods fail. But when someone does step up, neighborhoods succeed. You being that person: that's something substantive to be proud of, something that you can measure your own progress with. Your behavior will inspire others and remind them why they became a volunteer; your personal achievements will inspire yourself and remind you why you started.

HEALTH

BE HEALTHY, PROTECT YOUR STRENGTH

THREE YEARS AGO, in the summer of 2015, I felt rundown. Working extremely hard, I'd taken on a challenging lifestyle. In a drastic cycle, I ran around Chicagoland most evenings to fundraisers, dinners, and receptions and filled the rest of my nights sitting around on the couch. On those nights I'd work on projects next to my wife as she watched TV, mindlessly grazing on junk food.

Half of what led to the degradation in my health was the stress of over-working, and half of it was my decision-making and my own ignorance of what the right health choices meant.

Bottom line: I suffered the consequences. I gained weight, more weight than I'd ever wanted to. My habits began to take on a momentum of their own and I was losing control. I didn't feel like myself and I definitely didn't look like the person I wanted to be.

One morning, I woke up and I made a decision. I was not going to live this way anymore. I'd change my approach to my personal health and I'd get well.

I'll talk more about specifically what I did at the end of the chapter, but I'll tell you now that it will be some of what you've heard before. The broad categories that will help you change your life and lead to success on your own health journey are healthy eating, exercise, and stress reduction: familiar territory for anyone who has heard about improving health. But the approaches that you'll hear from some of the health professionals who have been on my show will be novel. Additionally, some work on motivation will first be necessary to ensure you stay on track.

Many tips will be up to you to personalize and customize, but you'll see that the advice they have to give can be integrated into your life and will give you results.

So let's dive in.

When first I decided to turn my health life around I personally worked with an expert in fitness, Albert Ferguson, a trainer who runs the Fitness Matrix in Evanston, IL. He focuses on personal training but also runs group classes and boxing instruction, bringing many people successfully to their fitness goals.

On my podcast, Albert gave some great tips on staying motivated. He recommends incremental change—instead of trying to focus on everything at once, concentrate on one area. Ensure you make the change in this one area slowly and give yourself enough time. "Don't do everything all at once, because the likelihood of collapse will [increase]." It takes 21 days to make a new habit; don't expect that change will happen more quickly.

At the same time, it's difficult to stay motivated on a six-month goal. Albert recommends setting up an 8-week token system where if you stay on target, you reward yourself with points. Let's say your goal is to reduce your portion size by twenty five percent. Every day that you do that becomes a token. If you have 50 or more tokens by the end of eight weeks you reward yourself with a night out on the town.

Above all: "Commit yourself to the process and you will see results," says Albert. When you see points adding up and others—family and friends—are seeing what you are doing, and encouraging you, that can also lead to greater motivation. By the time you hit the halfway point, you will see your own progress and that can also keep you going. He also doesn't recommend comparing yourself to others as a way of stimulating motivation— it can act as a distraction from the real goal of "being the best self you can be and to having the energy for the people who you love in your life."

Once you have strong guidelines for making health improvements in your life and feel confident that they will keep you motivated throughout your health journey, pick a first area to focus on in those categories mentioned earlier.

Andrea Metcalf, a nationally-sought-after celebrity fitness and nutrition expert has some good advice if you want to start by changing your eating habits. You can first change the composition of your diet. "The basics have always been the same—healthy eating: lots of fruits and vegetables." She told the story on the podcast of a woman who lost 25 pounds on the 47 banana a day diet—she only ate bananas! She doesn't recommend that, but—"Fruits and vegetables—you cannot go wrong," True vegans, she mentioned, only have a six percent obesity rate. Clearly, when your mother told you to eat your vegetables, she had the right idea.

Andrea says that in the eighties there was the low-fat diet, then low sugar, now paleo, and next will be high fiber and high protein. Despite all the trends, you don't need a complicated diet to lose weight. A study was conducted comparing the DASH diet, a complicated, detailed diet to lower hypertension and the high fiber high protein diet. What the researchers found was that followers of the high fiber diet made comparable gains to the DASH diet even though the DASH diet was more complex and difficult to adhere to. So you don't actually need a complicated diet to accelerate your weight loss. "25 grams of fiber—that's a lot of fruits and vegetables— [and] you will be healthy and have a trimmer waistline."

If you're a business owner, Andrea encourages putting out healthy foods (especially fruits and vegetables) for your employees to foster healthy eating."It's a small cost, but it goes a long way in helping them thinking about their day and their eating habits." Forget the vending machines—they only add a cost to your employee's waistline and to their pocketbooks. Instead, put out a basket of apples and charge a quarter. Give the money to charity: "Your employees [will] feel good about themselves."

Realize that it's a great boon to have that benefit that you can give to your employees. In addition, surrounding yourself with fruits and vegetables in your workplace will also help you in your fitness goals and give you social support to eat well during the day.

Something else that will help in your personal goals—somewhat counter intuitively—is moderation. Andrea preaches moderation as an integrated part of, and a reward for, eating well. It's okay to let loose once in a while, and to have a slice of Bundt cake with your gym buddies. As long as you stay focused on your overall nutritional goals, moderation can help with normalcy.

Albert Ferguson discusses two additional aspects of healthy eating: education and personalization. He believes "people need an education that will help them learn what they should and shouldn't be eating." Some people tend to eat for calories, but in the Fitness Matrix, he helps people eat for nutrients. As fitness and nutrition are intertwined, when clients come to see him, he gives them nutritional guidance that they can use as they train.

What Albert says demonstrates the value of trusted resources in your health journey—you can't make the right choices if you don't know what they are; this applies to nutrition just as it applies to fitness.

Albert makes his second point: the understanding that nutrition "is not a one-size-fits-all proposition." He says, "Different people depending on their schedules should eat different[ly]."

If you are a 9-5 professional, you can't expect to eat in the same way that a college student or an entrepreneur would. Don't put pressure on yourself to make particular food choices if the acquisition or preparation doesn't work for your schedule . Maybe you don't have the time to make a big salad every day for lunch—grab some almonds and an apricot and eat it on the go to your next meeting. Stay aware of your time limits andeducated about nutrition so you can make the right decisions throughout the day based about what you can realistically do.

One school of nutritional thought offers an alternative to the prevalent three-meals-a-day philosophy that could be useful to you as you adjust your personal nutrition plan to your schedule. The idea involves breaking up your eating, not into three large chunks, but six or more small meals a day.

Evolutionary logic bolsters this eating pattern. As humans evolved, they didn't have the bounty of food that we do—they ate when they could in the small amounts that they could find. As a result, the body burns food more efficiently when eaten throughout the day in smaller amounts.

Not a stricture—just another guideline that can be used in personalizing nutrition.

Another guest on my show, Luis Aruaz, consults companies on developing cultures of mindfulness and wellfullness. He recommends including food that will keep you satiated: "What I look for is the foods that are going to be the most energy that you need to carry you throughout the day the longest." Obviously if you feel satisfied you won't be as prone to binge eat! Those foods are "fats that will sustain you a lot longer than the average breakfast."

Luis explains the other benefits to fats:

Researchers are showing us how much sugar affects the brain and causes it to not work as well. Whereas, your brain is made up of 70% fat. If you are on a diet that doesn't allow for fats then guess what? Your brain is not working properly. Some of things to start looking at are avocados, egg yolks, walnuts, and almonds to allow the brain's actually work a little bit better.

So, to sum up, healthy eating means lots of fruits and vegetables, protein and fats: moderation, education, and personalization.

Next, exercise.

Albert recommends getting your exercise in early in the morning, especially for business owners. "That way, he says, "[you] can make sure no matter what comes up for the rest your day, you already have your fitness in. I'm sure many of you have experienced this; meetings, business work, and other interruptions can come up during the day and—-even if you are using my time management tips— exercise can fall by the wayside. That's why it's better to start the day off right, and put first things first so that you ensure you're actually including fitness daily in your schedule.

Additionally, the endorphins (hormones that produce positive feelings) that exercise produces can give you an energy boost that last throughout the day. If you put the bulk of your exercise until later, you miss out on that initial sustaining energy boost.

Even twenty to thirty minutes can make a big difference, says Albert, if that is all the time you have. Such a small amount of time looks paltry compared to a two hour chunk. Albert contends: "There is an inverse relationship between intensity and duration." This means that if you only have 20 or 30 minutes, you can push yourself to the limits of your intensity and get the same benefits of working out a lower intensity for a longer time.

When you start your regimen, bear in mind that many people find it difficult to work out solo. It's possible, but you have to have some mental fortitude to come to the gym every day with no-one holding you accountable.

Albert advocates finding group classes—they can be less expensive than one-on-one personal training and you can find support in exercising with other people. Albert calls it "sharing sweat to sweat equity": friendly competition leads to comradery that leads to better, more consistent exercise.

But business leaders are (obviously) busy! You simply might not have the flexibility to put in the daily morning workout, even for a short period of time. Pushing for a more integrated alternative than that morning workout block, Andrea offers tips on how you can intersperse moments of exercise as you work and "sneak in those fitness minutes during the work day."

She terms one way "pacing your calls." When you get a phone call get up and move around! Walk and you'll be using time that you would otherwise be sedentary to exercise.

When one famous business leader, Steve Jobs, took his calls in this way, he modernized what Aristotle, Freud, and other famous thinkers practiced—walking to get the mind going. Ferris Jabr expressed this in his 2014 article Why Walking Helps Us Think in The New Yorker: "When we go for a walk, the heart pumps faster, circulating more blood and oxygen, not just to the muscles, but to all the organs—including the brain." This represents one of the general daily benefits of walking as exercise, but can certainly help when working out business details on phone calls as well.

Go ahead and balance yourself off your chair as you work, says Andrea. It has roughly the same effect as balancing on a bouncy ball except your coworkers won't pass it around the office and play with it. Taking these short breaks and lifting yourself off of your chair to gives you a good upper body workout, even as you stay in front of the work you still need get done. Or set your timer and just stand up for a few minutes, getting blood to the legs and lower body and helping with circulation. Remember the 10 minute rule, if you walk for 10 minutes before or after meal "you've got your thirty minutes of exercise under your belt."

Anything you can do to get up and move around during the day, you should do. Uncross your legs, go to another office every hour, and get up to use the printer. It all adds up. And even if you don't get the workout in the morning, those short bursts of activity will still give you boosts of endorphins throughout the day.

The two methods Albert and Andrea discuss will give you the flexibility you need to utilize exercise depending on your schedule. Either way, the health benefits of exercise—endorphins, weight lose, an immune system boost— are worth the time investment.

If you've experienced continued stress, you know that it can have a significant effect on your health.

Luis Arauz entered the health field when his wife got sick. None of the doctors knew what was wrong, and they weren't helping her. With a background in science, physics, and computer technology, he started researching the problem.

He realized "There were higher root causes that nobody was talking about." Going deeper into the signs, he discovered these causes: inflammation and her inability to make energy.

So he shifted the thinking surrounding his wife's illness. He theorized that though the field medicine contained a wealth of research on the effect of stress on athletes and soldiers, not much thought focused on the effects of stress on business people who, unlike athletes or even soldiers, didn't get the opportunity for recovery periods after putting stress on their bodies.

Stress does have an evolutionary function; it would warn us of a dangerous predator or a hazardous change in terrain. Nowadays, the function of stress easily overloads into detrimental territory.

Those in business, especially entrepreneurs, can work up to 6 or 7 days a week and 365 days a year. According to Luis: "more and more business people waste their health trying to gain their wealth, and only to end up wasting their wealth trying to buy back their health." The prize of success comes at the price of increased stress with the end result being heavy health deterioration.

To combat stress, in addition to things like mindfulness (including meditation) and yoga, Luis advises regulating biofeedback - the signals your body gives to indicate your biological state—using a heart rate variability device. The small device is cost effective at less than a hundred dollars, clips on your ear, and measures your heart rate. If you are under stress the device turns one color, but when you reduce your stress it turns another. By focusing on using proper breathing technique (like the deep breathing techniques learned in a yoga class), you can reduce your heart rate and lower your level of stress.

Says Luis, "This device allows you to refocus and make sure that you are in that right mindset. So, that way you can maintain full focus and you can maintain productivity." Eventually, you will learn control and reduce your overall level of stress—and that's a great way to get rid of a major threat to your health.

I can personally say that by using many of these tips these health professionals offer, and by working one-on-one with Albert, I saw tremendous benefits. My waistline shrank, I felt healthier and happier, and I developed energy levels and productivity like I'd never seen before.

Albert told me: "The most important thing is limiting bad habits, picking up good habits." That's really how I started to turn my life around.

My wife and I began going for walks every day. I started doing exactly what Andrea suggested and walking during phone calls. I took it so far as to limit the number of in-person meetings I did so that I could convert them to phone meetings and walk (I purchased a great Bluetooth headset). People can see me these days at Old Orchard mall walking around, conducting business.

If I'm at a reception, I don't eat the hors d'oeuvres just because I can. I certainly don't sit around eating pretzel chips like I used to. I managed to balance what I eat—making smarter eating choices—and I did it without too many painful limitations. In fact. I eat tons, plenty, maybe more than I've eaten before. I eat those essential fruits and vegetables and in general I'm more conscious about what I eat.

I have a treadmill desk at home and, often when I'm at home and working, I'll be walking on my treadmill desk. I run every day in the morning. I ran my first marathon in October 2017 and I climbed up 94 flights of stairs for the Hustle Up the Hancock. Three times a week Albert and I work on strength training; we've developed a routine that helps me stay focused and a relationship that keeps me committed.

You'll be able to see much of this chapter's advice in my own regimen. I don't use everything these experts give, but what I do works for me.

Changing my lifestyle resulted in additional benefits that are separate from health, but nonetheless help in my life. Walking every day with my wife means that I can spend more time with her. Many of my phone conversations that I have while walking turn out to be more productive and more focused than typical in-person meetings. Being on the treadmill in the morning became a convenient way to fit in watching the news. So much good that I didn't expect came from changes originally made to protect my health.

I'm confident that if you stay goal-oriented and slowly switch out bad habits for good ones, then you'll succeed in your health journey. What works for you may not work for everyone and that's okay. Be kind to yourself; figure out the best advice from this chapter for you. No matter where you are, you can make improvements—you can be healthier. I've done it; I've seen the change in myself.

Be healthy and live a better life.

SMALL BUSINESS

COMING TOGETHER, BRINGING LIFE TO THE ECONOMY

WHERE ENTREPRENEURSHIP IS A PHILOSOPHY, a creative planning approach to stimulating business or community, small business is a method for building community and business. In small business, the goal is bringing people together; as many chambers of commerce as there are, as many other community non-profits, there's always more that can and should be done. In particular, in the communities that I am so passionate about,, there are so many synergies that have yet to be explored.

Individual businesses may operate in a silo but still have much to benefit from working together. The computer technician that is hustling, trying to reach people, should connect with the copy store down the street that could use his services. The fruit vendor who should connect with the natural ice cream shop two buildings over—all of these connections are made close to home, in a way that is naturally synergistic for the neighborhood.

When I entered the world of small business, I discovered quickly that it's great to advertise online, in the newspaper, on billboards (all things that work to some extent), but working together in person can more directly help people tackle mutual small business challenges. While small businesses don't have access to the same capital as large corporations, we can learn from how each of us have solved challenges like hiring and firing, managing finance, and finding vendors. All small businesses have much in common, and if we can build a community in which people could get to know each other, we would all benefit. We could find ways to work together, to exchange information, learn overlapping skills sets, and we could learn from our mistakes and successes.

The motivation to learn from everyone engaged in small business became part of the impetus for starting Jewish B2B. I would bring in different speakers that we all could learn from; even companies that were in competition with each other could come together and get stronger through the information brought by the speaker. Overcoming challenges became more important than reinforcing divisions, and I saw small businesses build a more synergistic community before my eyes.

My experience from my small family business, Moshe Klein and Associates, allowed me to teach other businesses how I had conquered challenges that they were just now encountering. I put on a number of workshops and a class called "How To Run a Small Business" in Illinois that we put on quarterly and featured diverse panelists—a lawyer an accountant a banker, a marketer. They gave speeches and provided advice; everyone that spoke agreed to do a free consultation with any small business owner in attendance. I heard a lot of positive feedback from this program.

I can't actually measure the results of every introduction I've made, every workshop we've put on. But even today I walk into restaurants or coffee shops and, see a meeting and say, "I introduced them!" They are working together, two business people sharing ideas, and planning their next project together. I feel rewarded. I know that hundreds of small businesses had been opened and come back from the brink because of our efforts.

Jewish B2B has made a massive impact on the business community; but as things have improved with the economy, as I mentioned in Jobs, we've taken a step back. I've found that I don't need to be the one to put on every event, or provide all the resources. While there was a great need to drive that change in 2010, these days I create that climate using other means. I chair the economic development commission in Skokie, helping businesses in that city connect with each other to attract and retain business; I do the same thing for West Rogers Park through JCCWRP.

I've witnessed many success stories from my efforts in building synergy between businesses and between small business owners and job-seekers.

There's a kosher restaurant in West Rogers Park that wanted to expand but was held back by financial problems. The owners were struggling; in order to generate more business they needed to beautify the storefront and improve their signage,—which would eventually lead to further expansion.

I introduced them to a small business consultant who had worked with the City of Chicago. Just a few months later, he got them approved for a small business grant, one that could that could get them over the monetary hurdle to expansion. The consultant reached success for his client, the business improved its storefront, and its signage—making the business and the city more beautiful—and the business grew. Win-win-win.

A success story for both a small business and jobs: a nursing home owner in the Jewish community was looking for a COO; I knew a job-seeker that had been operating a smaller business but was underemployed. I connected the two. Now the nursing home has a new COO; he is now making a great living, improving the business daily and more than fulfilling the requirements of the position.

Stephen Schwart, a long-time Skokie businessman, owned a small equipment broking firm called JM Scott. The business had been floundering. I was approached by the AAA motor-club, who was interested in opening offices in Stephen's neighborhood. AAA operates as a franchise model; they help business owners run their own branches. Stephen met AAA representatives through one of our Jewish B2B networking events. He opened a brand new AAA office and began employing multiple people. He now runs a successful small business that helps his customers directly with insurance needs and helps his neighborhood to thrive through the commerce he generates. Stephen went from struggling in his employment to building a business that has been successful for many years.

Though synergy can certainly fuel success stories, many elements of a business exist apart from synergy: starting the business, making decisions, attracting clients. Small business owners must do these tasks independently and with people they trust in order to build an effective business in a competitive business environment.

I've been involved in every role with my family business. At MKA, when I came into the business, we had a few people working for us. We grew slowly; in the beginning we had to figure out everything on our own. There's no manual to teach small business owners how to be successful when they get started. I'd been doing my dad's invoicing since I was 13, but when I formally joined the business, my role expanded and my dad tasked me with developing many strategies for growing the business. Every dollar was crucial; I researched more options for invoicing and found a service that would save us an extra five dollars a month on the invoices we processed.

We needed to create a website. The first website we built was a Go-Daddy account that cost only five dollars a year for hosting; otherwise it was a completely free platform. We've since upgraded the site and pay more than when we first got started, but finding that initial solution helped us get on our feet. We wanted to manage an email account and chose -Google apps because it maximized our resourcesand had a simple setup and low cost.

I made all these decisions myself. I had to make them on my own because there was nobody else to make them for me. When you are a small business and you work with a limited budget, you can't afford to hire twenty people to work out every detail. It might be ten PM but you still need to stay and choose your email account. No one will be there to choose it for you and if you don't make the decision yourself another day will pass and your business will be without email. .

Other than small-scale operational decisions, you need to make more general decisions: will I invest in technology or advertising? Will I concentrate first on further hiring or getting clients with the human resources I have? You must formulate plans to attract clients and to service the clients you bring in. As the business grows, you have to develop a strategy for how to scale the business— decide if and how you will reinvest in the business or whether you will reward yourself by taking a check. The time may even come when you need to decide you want to sell to someone else.

Capital must be found. Steve Hall, the director of small business lending for non-for-profit lender LISK, provides capital nationwide for small businesses doing loans through the SBA Community Advantage Program and the New Markets Tax Credit Program. Organizations like his provide an excellent way to build capital in early stages of business growth.

One of the big challenges from getting funding from big banks, Steve says, is that most businesses need to prove they've been in operation for at least two years. His organization does business for troubled industries, but he is willing to use other criteria to fund loans: businesses that have thirty-percent equity injection, solid business plans, andcommitment to growth over time. They are in the people business—looking for non-for-profit community and business leaders that have a true story about commitment to their community and family. They look for people who say "I've been working at this community restaurant for 20 years and I want to start my own," or a transportation company that says "I need two more trucks so I can get a deal from Eli-Lilly to transport goods from Indianapolis to Chicago. This will get my son a job, send my daughter to college, and let my wife quit her job at the hospital."- These are the people that will get funding for their small business through lenders like LISK even if they can't get it from a big bank.

Getting this capital helps to break small businesses out of the early stages of growth, but before that point, there are a lot of balls to juggle. Every day is different and it takes a lot of prioritization and organization to learn to develop the right instincts and trust in your own abilities. With very limited resources—limited capital, a limited number of employees, not much knowledge— you have to make the business work. Limited capital and employees are always givens when starting a small business, but many small businesses don't even know what interview questions to ask when hiring. They may even up asking bad questions and hiring the wrong person. All these problems can be fixed: capital can be found, employees can go into better roles, and knowledge can be acquired with experience.

Time, however, is the least growable yet most important asset any small business owner has. Because of the other limited resources you need to work fast before you've run out of the other resources and figure out the best use of your time. Manage your time and don't waste it on the non-essential—that way you can prevent your business from crashing before you've even started. You may be faced with many weekend meetings, but every business owner must make hard sacrifices if they want to see their business thrive. On the other hand, you'll benefit from the flexibility that ownership of your own time gets you.

Internally, there is no-one else who will own your business for you. No one would give it the same care and the same attention that you would, no one will do it as well as you can. The advantage, the luxury, and the challenge of being in business for yourself is that you own every piece of it. Every day that you aren't at the business is another day that you aren't making money servicing your clients. However, every day that you put in at the business, every effort you make, every success you achieve— for those things, you and only you deserve the ultimate credit.

Even though, as Small Business Association Deputy Administrator Marie Johns says,"Small businesses are the engine of our economy and the backbone of our community," the world that we live in makes it hard to work with small businesses. From the consumer perspective, you have to purposely intend to support these businesses in order to follow through on supporting them. When you Google a product, the big store options will be given to you, but the small store options won't. When you search for an accounting firm Moshe Klein and Associates won't pop up. You have to intentionally seek it out by searching for "small accounting firms in Skokie"; then you'll get the results you want.

I work around Google in this way all the time, and frequently, people will call me looking for a personal recommendation of a small business to work with. I can make that recommendation, benefiting both parties by helping them avoid the onerous sifting process that an internet search would entail.

I'll admit, I do have an Amazon prime membership. I wouldn't say I'm proud of it, but the reality is that sometimes convenience out rules the time it takes to support a small business. Though, in general, when someone uses small business, they will ensure that the store on their corner stays occupied and not empty. They'll keep that corner vibrant. That's why I make an effort to improve the resources that are out there that are helping people find small businesses, and advocate politically for small businesses themselves. Ultimately, using these resources and shopping and these stores will help local neighborhoods, people in your community, and even state and national economies. Small businesses create jobs—

that's a fact; they help people support their own families and put food on the table.

This is my advice to any consumer: shop at a local store. If you go shopping twice a week, make one of those trips to a local grocery store. If you need a product or service, don't always use the quick and easy big box stores that pay for the most prominent advertising online; shop small and shop local.

At the same time small business owners can't just rely on pity; they have to work hard to make sure that they stay front and center in the eye of their local neighborhood. They need to stay involved and give back in gratitude the effort that local customers give them when they shop at their stores. It's not easy to be a small business owner, but it's also not easy to be a consumer that makes the effort to shop at a small business. Both sides need to nurture the relationship to promote the best interests of themselves and their neighbors.

Still, why can't the world still exist without small businesses? Big box stores still provide jobs, they still support local economies, and they make things much easier for consumers and sometimes even business owners.

Jason Jacobsohn, a small business advocate with Alumni Ventures group, business advisor for Goldman Sachs 10,000 small business program, and leader of the Founders Institute, says that small businesses have an unrivaled nimbleness based on convenient features: great selection of products, better hours, local sourcing, and, personalized service.

Convenience is more complicated than it appears. While it may seem inconvenient to support small business, often it's actually more convenient. Even though shopping at stores like Amazon save you from having to leave your house, it may be that the items that you can buy at local stores are so specialized that you have a snowball's chance in hell of find them on Amazon or any other big box store. You'd have to do several internet searches—a whole lot of excess research—just to find the right descriptor for the item you need even though you have a picture of it in your head.

A local store could have that item so close by you can get it on short notice, even the same day, without having to worry that you won't have it when you need it. Many small businesses stay open when they are most needed or could even stay open for you; these businesses answer to the store owners and to their hours—not those set by corporations.

Local shops often already focus on a high degree of localized product synergy, so that you can try high-quality products from many places around your neighborhood and your city by shopping local. Your favorite coffee place might also sell bread from that amazing bakery around the corner you just heard about; it may bring in kids from the local elementary school to sell their art to give back to the homeless shelter. These types of amazing collaborations just aren't possible with large chains—they lack the flexibility and creativity that these small shops have.

Small businesses also give their customers a very high level of personal attention—you just won't find a personal touch at the alienating chains that have high levels of turnover and strict protocol for how employees treat customers. If you give a small business a phone call and want to reach the same person you did the last time—say if you are putting in a grill at your house and want the employee who installed it last year to give it upkeep this year—you need to support small business because only they can guarantee such consistency in service. If you always use that Amazon search, eventually that local shop will be out of business, and you'll be stuck without anyone to talk to about important purchases.

Shop at the local grocery store, or the local book store, or the local hardware store even on the days when you don't necessarily need them so that on the day when you really need them, they'll be there. It may cost you a few dollars more, but these are the people that know you, live where you do, and work with you. Big companies don't necessarily hire in your community, they'll post jobs online and people will come from wherever to get those jobs. Additionally, small businesses likely help people who initially need these jobs the most. "Small businesses are the largest employers of first time employees, people just out of college, and those returning from the military," says Steve Hall. These are the people that will continue to support the economy as they assume larger roles; it's important to get them into stable employment quickly.

Big companies don't necessarily treat their employees well—they're just out to make a buck no matter what it takes. Shop local, and residents who work at these stores will come to your neighborhood events and will become your friends because they can keep their job and stay in your neighborhood.

"Small businesses create two out of every three private sector jobs in our economy," says Marie Johns, "today, over half of all working Americans either own or work for a small business." It should be obvious by now how important it is to support small business, and if you are a small business owner, how important it is to set yourself up for success so you can start being a pillar of the local economy and community. Synergy is essential to any element of business success, but the motivation and spark to get a group of people together and build something is the start of drawing the right people and the right resources toward you. Support a small business, keep that spark growing. Start a small business, and watch it light up your neighborhood, your family, your country.

EDUCATION

OVERCOME YOUR BARRIERS, ALWAYS LEARN

I AM A LIFELONG LEARNER. I've pushed myself to become knowledgeable in areas that aren't necessarily easy for me. I've done hard work to acquire formal knowledge of education and of teaching. Nothing has come naturally. I've sweated over polishing my research skills, my academic writing, and my data collection ability. Pursuing my own education proved to be complicated, but in large part has made me the person I am today.

My ultimate purpose in completing my journey and finishing my doctorate in Educational Leadership is to encourage another next generation that education, while not the only way to achieve your goal, is incredibly important. Education is a way for many to get to their dream career path. It's a way for life-long learners to pursue knowledge, to network, and to associate with like-minded people that you can learn from. I've met some of the best and closest people of my life through education.

The first question I ask each job seeker I meet with, as I say in Jobs, is "What is your dream job?" Instead of saying, "I want to attend school here and here and here and then get my job," I tell them to start with the job and work backwards. No one size fits all in education. Not everyone needs to get a Masters, a Doctorate, or even a Bachelor's. There's a different career path for each person to get to their dream job, so everyone needs to first be clear on where they want to end up before they chose an education that will get them there. That way they can be precise about the right education for them.

People can be flexible in their pursuit of the right education to prepare for their dream job. I'm a big advocate of vocational education and trade schools. Many people I know have made a good living by attending these schools that don't require a traditional four year education.

That being said, there are no shortcuts. In order to become a doctor, you have to go to medical school; to become a lawyer, you need to go to law school. For people who have that goal in mind, it's about pursuing a rigorous traditional education. Even though no one size fits all, for every career path education, there's a way to get there.

Mentors also help immensely with pursuit of a job through education. Find people who have been in the same situation and they will be able to guide you to their goals, because they have already reached them.

Pursuit of knowledge guides my own educational journey, and relates to my overarching mission to help others. Standing in my office and looking at my wall, I see my degrees: my Certificate in Adult Jewish Learning and my Certificate in Arts Education and my Masters in Jewish Leadership. I view every opportunity as a learning goal. I look at opportunities like these and say, "Do I have a reason to say no?" I look at what I am doing in my life and say, "Do I feel knowledgeable enough to teach that?" Something that I do have the time for and don't have the knowledge in, I take on and learn. My lifelong goal is to be more of an educator. Not because I want to be a traditional teacher, but because I have been and aim to be a mentor to people. I view it as my responsibility, even at my young age, to learn from people and from traditional sources as much as I can. I'm not going to change careers and go to law school or medical school, but I go in for any opportunity to learn that I can because the pursuit of knowledge is intrinsically important and can make you a better teacher.

When I got my certificate in Jewish Leadership at SCS Northwestern, one of the major reasons that I joined the program is because I saw the diversity of people who were enrolling. It was fifteen to twenty people from the business world, the nonprofit sector, and the government. Despite the diversity of the student body, everyone was just like me: they also wanted to improve their skills, learn more, and get more involved in Jewish leadership. I realized I'd get to spend a year with these people in an interesting setting where we would be vulnerable, showing our real selves with equality and truth. That program was a game-changer for me; a new way to network aside from a happy hour, where I would see the same people week after week and learn about them on a different level.

I was blown away by that experience and by the people I spent time with. To this day they are my closest friends; I stay in touch and I talk with them all the time. My instincts about the cohort were true—we had a lot in common and we had similar goals in education. I've had the same experience and made stellar connections in every certificate and degree program I've joined. You are sure to meet like-minded people if you involve yourself in education. They could be a good networking resource, people that you can learn from, and friends that you keep for the rest of your life.

Education has many benefits, and you can get the most out of these benefits even if you had a problematic educational experience growing up. It's not your fault; education is in a difficult place right now. Due to widespread systemic deficiencies throughout the US, many people share the experiences I had all throughout elementary, middle, and high school. Alan Shusterman, Head of School for Tomorrow, says it's time to bring education into the twenty-first century: "K-12 education is an industry that has changed less than any other industry in this country," he says. "We're still preparing kids to enter the world as it existed in about 1980." Furthermore, the methods we use to teach kids are still based on an antiquated industrial-age model.

The American education system suffers greatly from these and other problems. It's not necessarily that other countries exceed us in education, although some countries like Finland and Australia certainly do thanks to their greater commitment to innovation. Though in this capitalist nation, where we are ahead of most countries in almost every respect and have shaped culture and commerce worldwide, we are, at best, middling in education.

In the era of innovation, America is stuck in the one-size-fits all model that, as I've said, I don't find effective. We move students along a conveyor belt, pushing them to hit arbitrary benchmarks that have nothing to do with what a student is really prepared for.

A few solutions exist to change the current state of American education. Customization is the better alternative to the conveyor belt method. Instead of classifying student by age and a general sense of intelligence, we would teach students with greater focus on the individual. This can be done by concentrating on the specific topic they are learning at that moment, at their current individual level, and in the pace and with the method that makes sense for that particular student.

American school systems could also use technology to revolutionize US education. Technology itself doesn't change learning, but, leveraged correctly, it can both change individual learning and our current model of education. In other industries, technology replaces lower-level tasks that workers would otherwise do; administrations can do the same thing in schools. Teachers would not have to focus on lesser tasks—they could teach using higher-level customization.

Of course, the world could benefit from the knowledge that education doesn't need to stop after high school. Such a mindset creates a way to mitigate the deleterious effects of early education by encouraging adults to continue their learning even if their childhood education wasn't beneficial.

Lou Falik, a well-regarded scholar-in-residence at the Feuerstein Institute, talks about MLE, Mediated Learning Experience, a process that can help in every stage of learning and throughout life. "It's a well developed carefully designed set of parameters," Falik says, "It's not a cookbook... based on recipes," but a customizable method. MLE is the way we teach people to understand more deeply the reasons for their decisions, why they think and act the way they do, and how to overcome blockages in their thinking or behavior. It's a proven way to make learning into a lifelong process.

One of MLE's central concepts is Structural Cognitive Modifiability, the idea that all people—no matter the age, no matter what kind of educational limitation—have the ability to be modified, not only in their behavior, but also in the structure of their brain. Everyone can create new neurons, new pathways, leading to an improvement and an acceleration in the way that learning is processed. We do this through the external behavioral examination that MLE offers.

An understanding of cognitive function, how you assess and gather information and use the information you've gathered to identify problem areas, can lead to better job performance and greater job-searching success. Tools—that will look like games to the non-initiated—such as crossword puzzles, sudoku, even games that we would play on our smartphones, can be gymnastics for the brain. People with educational limitations, e.g. those who lack the skills to concentrate, focus, or make decisions, can benefit from using these tools. Open yourself to the idea that learning is not restricted by age, educational limitations, or professional limitations, and be prepared to stretch your definition of what's truly educational.

I, myself, am an example of someone who overcame early education to succeed in higher-level education by overcoming obstacles on a non-traditional path.

In the Jewish community that I grew up in, I suffered from a poor education. I was bullied in school, even having to switch schools because of bullying. I was a good kid, the teacher's pet, on time and friendly; but I was never a stellar student.

I struggled my way through the system, finishing each grade and moving on to the next by miracle. I was still good at English studies because of the education my parents gave me at home, even so far as to test my older sister in reading and grammar in the car on the way to school. I suffered in Jewish studies, and though I was mostly okay in secular studies, I was just okay (especially in comparison to students at other schools) because the schools I went to couldn't provide solid instruction in any way. Period.

I passed through elementary school on to a high school that didn't provide any secular education. Again, I slid by during the three years I went. Again, the teachers liked me, but I didn't do particularly well.

After high school, I went to Israel. After Israel, then Detroit, attending a few different schools in both places. The schools in Detroit were technically colleges, but also lacked secular education, and though I gained some college credit for "Hebrew letters" it didn't provide a degree in the way most four-year colleges would have. That was fine with me; at that point, I aimed to be a rabbi and I thought that was all I needed.

Ultimately, my plan changed. I didn't become a Rabbi; I entered the world of public relations and took part in the family business. When I first came back to Chicago, I said, "I should really go back to school and get a degree." But I worried about how I would get my college credit back from the schools I went to after high school.

Eventually I got more involved in the community and established myself, building a reputation as someone who led business and volunteer activities and helped others. Any reason to go back to school fell by the wayside. So I dropped the idea.

I had started forming a community relationship for some of the programs at Spertus—they called me about a partnership they were forming with Northwestern University to create a Certificate in Jewish Leadership program. They asked me to publicize the program and I agreed, then they asked me to join the program. I thought "I don't need this, but the one thing that anybody can hold against me is that I don't have a diploma on the wall behind me." I said I'll do the Certificate and get a degree in a nice purple frame.

I completed the year-long program, learned a lot, met some amazing people, and had a fantastic time. Spertus then asked me to continue on to my Master's degree. I uncomfortably told them that I didn't have my Bachelor's degree. They were shocked. They knew me as a leader, running many events and programs in the community—they couldn't believe I'd gotten so far without a bachelor's.

They pushed to get me into the Master's, collecting my credits from the schools I'd attended, awarding me credits for my certificate, and granting me credit in recognition of my community work.

Then, for the second time in the history of the institution, Spertus awarded me an honorary bachelor's degree.

I finished my Master's from Spertus in three years. Once I'd gone that far, I decided to earn my doctorate in Education Leadership. At the time that I'm writing this book, finishing up my first year of coursework, and I'm investing considerable time working on my dissertation.

I went from no formal education to being very close to finishing a terminal degree. I'm proud of my commitment and my perseverance because there are no shortcuts; I know I earned my degrees and certificate through honest work. My journey is unique to me, but it was and continues to be of paramount importance because it will allow me to help people become better entrepreneurs, successful in their own path.

When my wife met me, she knew she was dating a guy with no Bachelor's degree. She saw everything I was doing in the community; the businesses I was involved in, and my entrepreneurship. But she saw me differently once I'd achieved my bachelor's.

We've been married for six years and it's funny to think about how we've seen the progression of my education together. My wife has supported me every step of the way. When we travel, she accepts the long hours spent working, the business calls that I go on, the writing for this book, and for the doctorate. I've told her, "After this, no more degrees." Luckily, she can trust me because there are no more degrees to earn. And she's relieved.

One more part of the story: Through the certificate in Jewish Leadership Program at Spertus, I got to know Michael Waitz, who worked for AEPI. Michael recruited me many times to speak many times at AEPI events to undergraduates, with the result that I was initiated as an honorary brother at their conclave at Bradley University at 2013. To this day I'm very involved in AEPI; I speak for them all over the country. So in the end, the guy that didn't have a bachelor's degree is getting his doctorate, and is a fraternity brother.

As I became an educator, many people began to benefit professionally from my instruction and my expertise on drawing resources from the educational world that I'd broken into. In my work through Jewish B2B, one of my goals was to make sure that job-seekers have the skills they need to be employable and successful in business. I brought in speakers to talk about how to gain the skills that would prepare them for the job: how to use Quickbooks, Microsoft Word, Microsoft Excel, PowerPoint, and how to build a LinkedIn profile. I've seen that people who have success in business or success on the job generally understand these different platforms. Instructing job seekers in these platforms during these (free) sessions would allow them to share in this success. For the JB2B business event, we also offered a wider range of helpful information both for job seekers as well as for business owners that would prove essential even for people who already had familiarity with the above-mentioned fundamental business platforms.

I've also been involved in many vocational education initiatives to help job-seekers. I'm a partner in Midwestern Career College; training people in health care.

One of my less successful attempts in business was a school I tried to found in Evanston that would specialize in vocational education. Being willing to spearhead initiatives like these, even if they fail, proves my passion for and commitment to vocational—and nontraditional—education.

I've seen a wide-ranging positive impact (that I've personally been told about) on the lives of individuals as a result of my involvement in education. My workshops in LinkedIn have led professionals to score business deals. My job clinics and my curriculums have improved job-seekers' resume and interview skills; they tell me that during specific job interviews they were able to answer a question better than they were before they attended the classes I gave them. Success stories like these make me feel rewarded and validated in my efforts.

My master's thesis was to create a job training program for Orthodox Jewish high schools. I set up a curriculum of guest speakers—including myself—to speak at schools like Hannah Sacks Bais Yaakov and Lubavitch Girls High School in West Rogers Park. Very recently, I was walking around at a grocery store and a girl in her early twenties came up to me and said,

"Do I know you?"

"Shalom Klein," I answered.

"You taught me," she said. "You taught my class three years ago."

It had been the first class of my curriculum.

"I have to say," she continued," because of the way you ingrained the importance of networking, I'm working right now. Because of you I focused on staying in touch with people. You gave me good advice and it helped me find a job."

I felt pretty darn good.

You will have your own unique educational path. Don't be discouraged by your past, your background, or your skill set. For every problem, you can learn the solution. Commit to becoming a life-long learner and the other benefits of education will quickly fall into place. With hard work, you will reach the point where you can teach others, and enjoy the satisfaction that comes with seeing others achieve their goals. Education will open doors; be the person to go through them.

RELIGION

BE A LIGHT UNTO THE NATIONS, BE A LIGHT UNTO THE WORLD

RELIGION ENDOWS MEANING to many people's lives. Personally, my wife, Elisheva, and I are committed to the Jewish faith. We practice Judaism in our own way. I find that more important than religious law, "*halacha*", are religious values, "*arechim*": inheritance, kindness, charity, creating a good example for others, and business ethics.

Inheritance of the Jewish faith reaches back generation upon generation, traditionally from receiving the Ten Commandments after liberation from Egypt. This isn't a value statement, especially not over the religions of others, but it does speak to the strength of Jewish values and the strength of those who kept Judaism alive, defying the pressure of time. I'm proud to be part of that tradition and to embody that strength.

My parents always let me religiously decide who I wanted to be; they never forced anything on me. However, they've always emphasized the importance of being a good person. My father never said "no" when people needed help. Working in finance, he helped people that struggled to manage their own finances and gave advice, not really writing a check but rather, helping them create a budget to ensure that they wouldn't end up back in their default situation. I remember my father accepting calls in the middle of the night, selflessly offering advice even at four o'clock in the morning because he knew how worried people could become about their finances. I don't help in the exact way my father did; I help people with resumes rather than with budgets. But his example demonstrated for me the importance of Judaism and the effectiveness of inheritance.

Jewish education also plays a major role in keeping inheritance alive. Without Jewish education, the values that I consider essential to creating a good society become lost. We believe in enhancing Jewish education and expanding it to reach all children so that we not only sustain it, but raise our expectations for it in the next generation that carries on our traditions and our heritage. We were privileged to receive the "Barney Goldberg Young Leadership Award" at The Associated Talmud Torahs (a society that focuses on Jewish Biblical education) 2015 Annual Gala for our vision and leadership. This award offers a testament to our continued commitment to Jewish education and has bolstered my own belief in my ability to pass on Jewish values to the next generation.

When my father helped those people all the years of my childhood and adolescence and, as he continues to do today, he keeps the Jewish value of *chesed*: kindness. Though I'm a big fan of *tzedakah*, charity, and as I've mentioned, I give every cent I can to Jewish organizations that help those in need, in some ways I find the value of kindness a more foundational Jewish value.

From a very young age, I heard my father quote Maimonides, the 12th century universally revered Jewish philosopher, in this regard: "Give a man a fish and you feed him for a day, teach a man to fish and you feed him for a lifetime." All cultures and all religions have some variation of this adage, but, for me, receiving this philosophy in the context of Judaism caused it to influence me and last with me until this day. More than simple monetary charity, *chesed* creates a sustainable situation in which people can thrive. I'm not a rich man, I can't endow organizations, but I can help others that are less fortunate by helping them become more independent professionally, and therefore, financially capable on their own.

Beyond the direct personal satisfaction and fulfillment that both parties gain from *chesed*, Judaism fosters a value that's an expansion of this ethic. Jews are meant to be "a light onto the nations," setting a shining example of goodness and truth for everyone they meet. I've prioritized publicizing my Jewish identity, bringing Judaism into the name of Jewish B2B Networking and the Jewish Community Council of West Rogers Park, because I believe that Judaism has been a direct cause of my ability to do good.

Of course, everyone can join any of my organizations, but I, in particular, want the positive role I play in my community and in the many I touch with my efforts, to be associated with the source from which that positivity stems: Judaism.

One of the people that I was fortunate enough to learn from when getting my Masters in Jewish Professional Studies at Spertus was Dr. Hal Lewis. My professor and faculty advisor and formerly the head of Spertus, he's written extensively on Jewish values and community service. Dr. Lewis has this to say about Jewish leadership, "Jewish leadership represents its own discrete discipline that has a great deal to teach those who serve in leadership capacities within and beyond the Jewish organizational world." Jewish leadership is unique and it derives that uniqueness in large part from the continued discipline of being a light onto the nations.

Every week I go on the radio and declare, "This is Getting Down To Business with Shalom Klein!" My name is Shalom Klein; a Jewish name that when people hear, have no question of mistaking who I am or the identity that I have. I'm up front about my commitment to the Jewish holidays; I'll say on the air that I won't have a live show this certain week because that's during Passover. I never hesitate to speak about my Judaism.

My efforts to bring my Jewish ideals to the business world have been recognized on the national level. On visits to the White House during the Obama Administration, I accompanied faith-based leaders (with whom

I'm sometimes grouped) from around the country to speak on the relationship between business, community, and religion. I've spoken in front of imams, rabbis, pastors, and ministers about how important it is for them to help their people in their communities find employment and to earn their own livelihood. Those visits were a responsibility and an honor; to have a seat at the table at which every religious leader contributes, to add my Jewish perspective, and be a role model of someone who can publicly express their religion in the business world.

As I travel, whether for business or pleasure, I make it a point to celebrate Jewish holidays with people of all faiths. If it's Passover, I'll hold a Seder. If it's Hanukkah, I'll light the menorah. On cruise ships, I've led a Seder for forty-five people and I've lit Hanukkah candles for one hundred. Whether we have Jews, non-Jews, or both, I'll teach a message during these ceremonies that everyone can find relevant.

It's touching to see the impact those moments of sharing can have on everyone involved. It might be strange to hear but I, like many of you, also enjoy Christmas time. I enjoy watching Christians celebrate: singing Carols in the streets, putting up Christmas trees, eating roast chestnuts with Santa Claus. Everyone celebrates Religion in their own way; even though I may not be a believer in the same things Christians believe, that doesn't bar me from enjoying the way that they celebrate. Similarly, my own faith-celebrations can include everyone, Jews and non-Jews, because I know that they could very well enjoy my holiday as much as I do.

Since I believe in the Jewish responsibility to be a light onto the nations, I also believe that it's important for every Jew to be involved in social justice, in human rights. I care about Israel and I care about my local Jewish institutions and organizations, but I believe that we shouldn't only defend our own issues and our own causes. In some ways, being involved in other communities, neighborhoods, and countries is just as, if not more, important.

When I get out there into those other communities and act as a Jew publicly because I know that it's both my obligation and the right thing to do, ninety-nine percent of the time I get a positive reaction. People admire that I can be so bold about this aspect of my identity and see the good that my expression of Judaism does for others. Between two religious people, this can be especially true: there's far more that we agree on than what we disagree on.

The other one percent of the time, when I face Anti-Semitism or anti-religious sentiment, I'm surprised because it's such an exception to the reception I get the vast majority of the time. I don't view the other person's reaction as a reflection on me or my Judaism. Usually the other person's viewpoint or upbringing has caused them to deviate from a generally accepted reality: being open about one's religious identity is a good thing, and respecting another person's religion is a prerequisite to respecting people themselves.

In terms of relating to others in the business world, one of my other guiding values has been Jewish business ethics. Business ethics have such a huge focus in Judaism that I would say that the business ethics we have today come from Jewish tradition. Two whole tractates of the Mishnah, the original first century codification of Jewish law, concern nothing but the laws of commerce and many other examples abound throughout the rest of those books. The abbis of this period built these laws after the laws of given in the Five Books of Moses, the urtext of the Jewish people. For hundreds of years after the Mishna, later Rabbis took part in an even more thorough discussion of commerce recorded in the thousand-page set of books, the Talmud. Many orthodox Jews study this daily so as to become sharper at reasoning in a variety of different real-life situations, including those involving business ethics.

Though many of the particular examples the Mishnah and the Talmud use—threshing in fields, situations involving the selling of oxen and sheep—wouldn't seem applicable today, many are. There are situations involving lending money, accurate weights and measures, verbal deception in trade, intellectual theft, and whistleblowing. Even concerning the examples that don't seem applicable, and certainly for the ones that are, principles can be derived that help immensely in navigating and staying ethical in today's world of commerce. Of course, learning about these situations and understanding the principles at work behind them as well as their proper conclusions relate back to the value of education which, as I've mentioned, I value highly.

Jewish business ethics helped me stay a good person and stay grounded. One of the founding principles in the Talmud is that if there is a business dispute, people shouldn't become involved in the messy gray area where the contesting parties—or those judging them—may make a mistake in the ruling between them, but rather, should draw a line prior to the gray. This keeps people away from problems that would be created through inadvertent error and doubt. Learning from this principle in particular has kept me honest in many of my own business dealings.

Personally, despite being very much a part of my identity, religion is less about observance and, as I've said, more about values as well as spirituality. In terms of spirituality, I prioritize respecting those parts of Judaism that allow me to have having a positive effect on the lives of others and on my own life.

Many observant Jews become very strict on keeping the minuta of Shabbat observance. I instead espouse the words of Abraham Joshua Heschel, one of the most prominent Jewish theologians and philosophers of the 20th century, who writes: "Strict adherence to the laws regulating Shabbat observance don't suffice; the goal is creating the Shabbat as a foretaste of paradise."

Heschel still advocated some observance to the laws of Shabbat; I take a still more liberal approach. For me, Shabbat is a time to slow down, to spend time with family, and eat festive meals with them. I don't regularly go to my own synagogue on Shabbat. But I don't look at my phone, get caught up in electronics, or involved with work. I unwind, I decompress, and that's how I observe. That conceives a space for me to create a vision of a future time when we will have the plenty to live together without needing to be so driven and non-stop. I relish those moments and view them as the cornerstone and the fuel for what allows me to do what I do during the week.

My personal understanding of spirituality, and the impetus to define my personal relationship to Judaism, is also something I inherited from my parents. We grew up in Vernon Hills. I was born there in the late eighties when that city wasn't particularly a hub of Jewish life. My parents moved to Skokie partially because of the Jewish schools and synagogues that thrive there, oriented to more of a strict observance of Judaism. Though my family moved to greater observance, one thing that remained consistent in my parents' house was prioritizing being good people and helping others.

At this point, my family has diverged in our levels of observance. My sister leads a more religious lifestyle than I do. After moving from Vernon Hills, then to Skokie because of community, my parents recently retired to Maricopa, Arizona where the nearest Jewish community is a thirty-minute drive away. I'm not a fan of labels: I don't believe in Orthodox, Conservative, Reform—the traditional divisions of the Jewish people. Despite our different understandings of Judaism, my family all respect each other and we're all just as Jewish because we all remain faithful to Judaism in our own way. My sister takes daily satisfaction in observing the laws, I in my values and spirituality, and my parents appreciate going to their own community more than ever. This is something that you can strive to approach in your relationship with family and religion: being understanding and accepting of all your family members' practices.

———

Rabbi Vernon Kurtz, the rabbi of North Suburban Synagogue Beth El of Highland Park, the president of the American Zionist movement, and formerly the Head of the Rabbinical Assembly was also one my Professors at Spertus and is a role model for me. He's talked extensively on the subject of reconciliation between Jewish practice and being a good person. Yes, he's said, he's a Rabbi and Rabbis are often associated with their level of observance. However, more than prioritizing practice, he aims to be a good person. Yes, prayer is important, keeping kosher is important, but people that say, "I pray three times a day and eat only certain foods," and bring that as sole proof that they are a good person are not being real with themselves or with other people.

Instead of going to synagogue, I walk with my wife almost every week on Shabbat to her grandmother's nursing home. Come Saturday morning, we walk there to participate in a brief service with their rabbi. Besides for this being good exercise, it puts a smile on my wife's face. That's a better way for me to be Jewish than to go to my own synagogue and my own rabbi; it breaks the insularity I'd otherwise develop and makes me a better religious person by being there for my wife's grandmother. In general, this illustrates the most important part of Judaism: being able to make a real change in how people enjoy and find meaning in their own lives.

In Passover of 2017, I was on a Seabourn cruise from St. Martin to Barbados. We lead a Seder for a nice handful of people. The Seder lasted only about two hours but it was beautiful. We sang traditional songs that everyone knew and everyone joyfully participated.

I was sitting next to a couple; the husband, Avi, was a holocaust survivor and showed me the tattoo on his arm. He talked to me about the cruise—he was having a rough time. He wasn't happy with the food, and with this, and with that.

My wife and I try to socialize with everyone, knowing that once we see a person at the Seder, everytime we go somewhere on board, we'll be identified. People will seek us out and schmooze with us for a few minutes as they enjoy their day.

I saw the man that I'd sat next to over the days following the Seder, making sure to touch base with him about whether things were improving. The last two days of the cruise I didn't see him, and since I'd seen him almost every day, I got worried about him. I went over to the cruise director and said I hadn't seen Avi in a while.

"Oh," She said, "he's in the medical center."

"What happened?" I said.

She couldn't tell me. "Go down and ask the doctor."

I went down and asked the doctor if I could come in. The doctor asked Avi who said "Yes, yes, yes—I want him here, I want him here."

Avi had gotten pneumonia and wasn't doing well. Eventually, he had to transfer to a hospital in Barbados. I sat with him, talked with him for hours while he was still on board. That was a very meaningful experience for me and his wife.

Avi passed away a short time later. His wife said through email that I had helped cheer him up. That Seder was the last one he experienced before he passed away. Knowing that I holding that Seder with him became a profound, happy experience before Avi passed away is a testament to my understanding and my practice of Judaism. When I think of Avi, I know that Judaism made that powerful moment between us; one that helped in the last part of Avi's life.

Up until this point, I've spoken extensively on interpersonal relationships in Judaism. There are two central relationships that Jewish people have: their relationship *"bein adam lechavero,"* between a person and his fellow, and their relationship *"bein adam lamakom,"* between a person and God.

I think about God every day. I don't go to daily prayers, but I put on tefillin—phylacteries—for two or three minutes every day and use that time to meditate and offer my personal prayers to God. I feel good doing this: being able to relate God to myself, to my family, and to my world. I have my own special relationship with God. It impacts my day and the way I feel about myself and about the entire world.

You can have whatever relationship you want with God; whatever relationship you want with your religion. As long as it benefits yourself and others, you will have brought light into the world. Be that light to others and be that light to yourself.

ENTREPRENEURSHIP

THINK CREATIVE, BE DECISIVE, SEE YOUR IDEA THRIVE

I'VE BEEN AN ENTREPRENEUR from a young age. Now I'm finishing my doctorate, but growing up I was never the perfect student. I preferred to learn from role models and by taking action in a nontraditional way, not how people told me to do things, but in the way that I felt things could be done. As I got older, this entrepreneurial spirit manifested itself in a wide-range of business and community endeavors. I began to see myself as an entrepreneur and other people could see the entrepreneur in me.

The classic definition of an entrepreneur is a business person who puts money into an endeavor, growing it and building it until it (hopefully) meets with success. For me, entrepreneurship isn't just about money and it's not just about time. It's not just about trying to profit off of a new business; a Mark Zuckerberg growing FaceBook.

Entrepreneurship is anything out of the box, anything where you take a risk, as I took risks when growing up. Challenging yourself and, at times, challenging others, departing from the norm and creating, shaping, and nurturing in a novel way. Whether in your business, non-profit, or personal life, you can take this approach and make yourself an entrepreneur by exemplifying the out-of-the box ethos, finding creative solutions, and taking risks. You'll find that by being willing to think in these ways and by adopting a broader definition of entrepreneurship, you'll succeed where others fail. You'll avoid inaction, you'll take on fear, and you'll foster an attitude that can conquer diverse challenges.

When you adopt this attitude, you'll not only break the classic definition of entrepreneurship, but you'll open yourself up to so many opportunities that you won't need to think of yourself just as a businessman, or as someone who works in non-profit, and other people will think differently of you as well.

Many people don't know how to categorize me. I'm involved in so many projects and I wear so many different hats that it's practically impossible for everybody to know everything I'm working on. I've asked scores of people "what do you think of when you think of me?" and I've gotten just as many answers. Though a significant number of people see me as an entrepreneur. They see that I'm involved in all of these endeavors and they see my work as a consultant, but in particular, they see that on any given day, I'm going to 18 meetings on 18 different subjects—and they say "he's an entrepreneur!" I'm okay with that. The truth is, that's closer to my own definition of an entrepreneur than the classic definition and that's closer to the truth.

Jeremy Smith a friend, entrepreneur, and the founder of SpotHero, shared advice on my podcast about keys to success as an entrepreneur. Entrepreneurs have a bias toward action; they push for things to happen rather than sitting around waiting for opportunities to come to them. They are proactive as opposed to reactive—they concentrate on preventing fires rather than just putting them out. Entrepreneurs are committed to improvement; they or their team may not be experts, but with commitment they work toward mastering the skills or tasks they need to get ahead. Successful entrepreneurs also have deep understanding of core problems in their field. "If you are intimate with a segment of the market it [becomes] clear where inefficiencies lie and where solutions [need to go]," says Jeremy.

Todd Heyden is the owner of Lock, a sports-tech company that runs a mobile app focusing on social and short duration fantasy game-play, a recent market that's primed for growth. His and his partner's impetus for starting Lock stemmed directly from wanting to solve industry problems. They themselves were avid users in the consumer fantasy game space, and they were tired of watching other people solve problems facing the industry that they knew they could solve. He and his partner had been successful in past endeavors, so they jumped in building their company as quickly as they could in the city of Chicago. As fans of video games themselves, they've been able to capitalize on a lot of their gut feelings about their platforms. These feelings are mostly accurate; they've been able to work off the solutions to the problems they solved initially, but they've also developed a greater feel for their consumer base as they've progressed.

"Fortune favors the bold," says Todd. In addition to the passion that's necessary at the start of any new project (as with pursuing jobs or growing an organization), you'll need to recognize that it's a rough road to start your own business or entrepreneurial project. Be ready for this challenge; be realistic about how much energy you'll have to put in and how much focus you'll need. That way you won't be surprised when the going gets tough—you'll be primed. You must also be willing to evolve and change—hard work, but work that will keep you in the market.

Todd Heyden and his company possess another major requirement for starting a successful entrepreneurial venture—clearly defined goals. "We hope that this app will be in hundreds of thousands of peoples' hands and then millions of people's hands." After running the platform through beta tests, developing the app, and putting off marketing for the first four months, he now has an action plan that will lead him to that goal: "It's time to scale this and rerelease the product for the start of the football season [because] as sports fans, people get excited for that August/September feeling."

Everybody works best at a different stage of entrepreneurship. Some thrive at the seed stage, some at the nurturing stage, and some at the high-level growth stage. I like to be high-level and work with people, which is why I thrive at external affairs, and avoid granular policy issues.

Jeremy's personal experience also mirrors this philosophy. He felt that he was much better adapted to help at the earlier stage where entrepreneurs need to hustle, get the initiative off the ground, and get the potential consumers excited about the product. The next stage of his business, dependant on developing and allocating venture capital, growing fast, and beginning to manage employees, wasn't suited to him as a young principal. These were unfamiliar skills; he recognized the difficulty of developing those skills under a tight development deadline and knew that others in his organization might be better suited to the task. "It's important for entrepreneurs to understand that," says Jeremy, "to get those requisite skill sets on the team in some capacity. You need to be the person to do that or [be the person] to get those skill sets on your team." You don't need to do everything, just make sure that the work gets done.

My own work is broad, but I still know my limits. As much as I stretch my capacity so that I can truly reach that definition of entrepreneur, I don't use this as an excuse to involve myself in tasks of which I have no expertise or no chance of success. I know what I do and I do it well.

Here's my definition of what I do inside of the umbrella of entrepreneurship: I assist companies and organizations with external affairs. I work with dozens of different companies, some of which I have a personal stake in, and others that I only consult for. I'm involved in everything that's not core business related. If they are a health-care organization, I'm not helping them with health care. The same goes with education, finance, or facilities, and construction. I get involved with everything else: public relations, technology, regulatory requirements, business development, media relations, and marketing. I have my radio show, and I sit on many different community boards. My work that I do for dozens of organizations, some for hire, some not for hire, some that I'm invested in personally, some that I'm not invested in personally, all falls within the limits of my capacity and my knowledge of my boundaries.

I also know that though I enjoy exploration, running around, and putting my energy in many different places. One day, I intend to commit myself one hundred percent to one of my projects. As much as breadth can be sustaining, a true businessman ultimately aims for success in depth. Right now, I also know myself and my preferences and I enjoy my this lifestyle; I am too passionate about the many things I do to give that up. You will also need to see how far you want to take each stage of your entrepreneurial journey and to figure out when (or if) you want to shift your style and commit to one business.

Being an entrepreneur and being involved in so many projects means that eventually, you will be involved with projects that don't get off the ground.

In 2015, I started a vocational school called The Career Institute. I had been approached countless times by companies—employers that were desperately seeking highly-skilled workers, to fill hundreds of open positions.

My partner and I sought to fill this need, creating an organization that would help people to find and train for these jobs, and get them into these employers' open positions. My plan was to put myself one hundred percent into the business. I was going to become the CEO, my partner the COO. We rented space in Evanston, we got approved by the State of Illinois to open a for-profit vocational college that would train people in health care.

Unfortunately, we miscalculated several things about the fee structure for the courses and this small error in judgment meant we had to close down even before we held our first class.

It was not fun. My wife had helped me every step of the way. She and I had already decorated my office space in anticipation of our opening. We put in hundreds of hours and a lot of money into an idea that didn't end up happening.

I did get involved in another school, a very similar model that I invested in and now consult for called Midwestern Career College. But the sting of that failed business venture didn't depart just because I'd made the idea live on in a different form.

However, every cloud has a silver lining. The doors that I've opened (with Midwestern Career College as well as other vocational schools) and the opportunity to learn from failure benefit me until this day.

You can't let the failures prevent you from starting new initiatives. You can't get bogged down in the past as an entrepreneur. Looking to the future and staying involved and excited keeps your outlook healthy—endowing your existing businesses with energy and purpose. One of the best things about being an entrepreneur is being able to start new ventures. Don't lose the good feeling you get each time you do; hold on to it and bring it to the next project regardless of eventual success or failure.

I had a moment of realization in India in December 2017. I'm asked all the time by people about my trips: "Where have you been, how did it go, who did I meet with, tell me about your experiences, how did you make that happen?" Working off of the excitement about my travel I saw around me, I decided to start something new. I'm partnering with a friend of ten years, Becky Adelberg, to start an organization that will allow people to live my travel experiences. Becky and I are launching a travel business where we will have several annual experiences focused on entrepreneurship. We'll help entrepreneurs meet potential colleagues in different countries around the world—we've already planned visits to India and Thailand. We have the price points knocked down to rock bottom and we've brokered high-level meetings that most people wouldn't be able to set on their own. Between us, we have the makings of a successful for-profit business, fueling my light-bulb moment into an entrepreneurial venture. That, for me, is very exciting; a rewarding piece of being an entrepreneur.

As you can see from the above story, much of what makes me an entrepreneur is that I don't just get involved in entrepreneurship for myself. Instead, I've tried to help others on their journey to becoming an entrepreneur, whether in business or in community. We all need advice. Even two businesses that look similar can have different concepts or different needs, and better advice is specialized to each business.

Adam Fridman was at a networking event and he met with a litigation attorney who was there to give free advice. "It was a shocking revelation," says Adam, "that someone with that stature from such a big firm was there to give free advice." He thought how many entrepreneurs are looking for that free advice, for that support and those resources to help them in their goal to start a small business? On the flip side, how many experts are looking to share that free advice?

These questions led him to start Meet Advisors, an organization that Forbes coined "The Yelp for Entrepreneurs." The concept is simple: pick an advisor you like, ask a question, leave a review. It's about bringing people together, but it's also about a free exchange of the material that helps every entrepreneur progress.

Adam Fridman considers advice an essential foundation for those hoping to start their own company: you need to start with the checks and balances gotten from others around you. He himself is passionate about any projects he starts: "When I lock onto something, it's my baby." However, he advocates checking with people who have been in your shoes before so that you have the flexibility to pivot before you start your venture. Entrepreneurial journeys are expensive and resource intensive; you need to get advice from individuals or any number of the support organizations available to give yourself the information you need to avoid pitfalls and succeed. From another perspective, if your venture isn't a good idea, you need to hear that so you can sidestep years of wasted effort, and invest in something that you can bring to success.

Adam has witnessed many success stories from Meet Advisors where advice has helped to conquer many challenges. In Naperville, a company called Commercial Lending that had been growing very fast faced a legal dispute with a client that had the potential to derail growth—they simply weren't ready to spend the money to get the support to solve the question. They reached out to an attorney via Meet Advisors and received an answer within twenty-four hours and were then able to pivot their dispute with the client while minimizing their future risk of getting paid. They subsequently hired the attorney that helped them and built a fruitful relationship.

"What was amazing," Adam says, "was how quickly they received a response, how quickly they were able to pivot, and get to what's next." The advice they received, and the speed with which they received it, proved crucial in helping them past a major challenge to their future as a company.

At some point, however, you need to break free from advice so that you don't rely on it like a crutch. The farther you are along in the process, the better, but you also need to learn from your own successes to minimize your mistakes. Meet Advisors offers a framework for giving your own advice; you can switch to that side once you become an expert in your entrepreneurial field. That way, you contribute to a more informed field and a more trusting environment to do business.

More than just advice, the ability to successfully network and build connections with people can be indispensable to building any business. Clearly this is my specialty—I'm someone who works best at higher level external affairs—but I can also help in every step in building a business, from getting seed money, to nurturing clients, to gathering more clients.

One of my role models as an entrepreneur, a mentor to me on many levels, is Avi Goldfeder. Avi was the Chairman of Pharmore Drugs, but because of sheer magnitude, I will never know everything he is involved in. He's successful in business, successful in politics, and successful in community. What sets him apart from everyone else and what does he do better than anyone I've ever met? He connects with people. An inveterate schmoozer, a winer and diner, the fact that he can talk to anyone brings incredible strength to his efforts as an entrepreneur and has led to incredible success.

The most attractive thing about entrepreneurship is ownership. The most entrepreneurial project that I'm involved in today, even though it's not a traditional business, is the work I've started with Jewish Community Council of West Rogers Park. I'm taking this initiative that was completely dormant before I got involved and putting in enormous amounts of time and effort, using every possible relationship and connection I have to bring people together. Jews, Indians, and Muslims are collaborating to open businesses in a neighborhood that needs to be revived. This is a fresh idea, one that I wake up thinking about, saying, "How can I move the needle forward?" and one that I go to sleep still thinking about saying, "What's next?" This is an idea that I've seen through from the beginning and nobody else owns it but me. That's ultimately what entrepreneurship is: taking ownership of an idea and taking it to the next level.

When you work a job, you don't possess ownership; you do what somebody tells you to do and then you go home. That's not right for many—a lot of people don't just want to stress about work; they want to focus on how their projects will live on. Adam Fridman started out in the finance field, but he wasn't happy with a nine-to-five; he was passionate about creating. This led him on a ten-year journey, but he's happy he went through it because now he owns what he created.

Every day looks different as an entrepreneur. One day, it's one challenge, and the next day, day it's another challenge. One day, things are moving and flowing, and other days, things don't go as planned. But every day you get to meet people, to problem solve, to see the fruits of your labor. You know that after a successful meeting or initiative you can say "I did that." These days, there are buildings that I can point to and say, "I know that as a result of my being involved, that building is up." I can see someone and say, "Since I was involved in that person's job-search, he has a job." That's a pretty darn good feeling. And that's the beauty of entrepreneurship.

JOBS

NETWORK WITH PASSION, GET YOUR PERFECT JOB

AT FIRST, I HAD NO IDEA what networking was. People told me I needed to network for my business so I started going to networking events, talking to people, and getting better at making connections. I began to realize the effectiveness of networking, and I got so enthusiastic about the concept that I decided to host my own networking event.

In June of 2010, I put on a networking event at the kosher Skokie restaurant Slice of Life, expecting twenty people. Seventy-five people showed up, and the event proved to be very successful. I started getting the feeling that events like this could form the framework of an entire organization.

The next day, I walked into my favorite Starbucks and saw four meetings going on, continuations of conversations between people from the day prior who had met at my networking event. At this moment in 2010, many people struggled to find employment. These conversations proved that networking held the potential to turn the situation around, as well as improve the economy by making connections between existing businesses.

I built the organization that I'd began to see the framework for— Jewish B2B Networking. We focused on establishing a comprehensive network, evolving from monthly networking meetings to having multiple events on a weekly basis: job clinics, business networking events, even a Shark Tank for entrepreneurs seeking funding and mentors for their business. We grew from events solely held on the North Shore of Chicago to holding events all over the Chicagoland area and even events in Washington D.C., Detroit and Milwaukee. We developed our network all over the Midwest and beyond. Jewish B2B Networking worked.

As our success grew I thought, "If we're getting one-hundred people at each of our events imagine if we could get everyone under one roof on one day. That strength would be phenomenal." We already had representatives going to Washington D.C. and Springfield advocating for more support for job creation from our government. We thought that this event could both make us better advocates and create an unprecedented networking opportunity.

The Jewish B2B Networking Business Event went from 2010 all the way until 2015. An all day employment and business expo, we had over one-hundred exhibitors and two tracks of workshops held every hour: one for business owners and one for job seekers, as well as a free job clinic. Each year drew more and more people. In the first year, we predicted that one thousand people would come. Twenty-five thousand people came. We held it in the Holiday Inn in Skokie, a popular and spacious venue for all types of events. We ran out of parking within the first few minutes.

We brought The Business Event to Lincolnwood, downtown Chicago, Drury Lane, and Oakbrook Terrace. At the high-point the event expanded to 5,000 people with massive amounts of jobs found and business being made just because of this one event. It formed a major touchstone of Jewish B2B networking.

Of course, Jewish B2B included many other events, but despite the number of activities hosted, it instituted a practice that set it apart from other organizations. Everything about Jewish B2B Networking was completely free—neither I nor anyone associated took a penny from it. We charged no money for any event unless on a rare occasion a dinner or lunch had to be covered. We ran on a one-hundred dollar budget, which came out of my pocket. Our only costs were email blasts on MailChimp and paper goods for our events. Venues were sponsored and oftentimes, food was sponsored. We had no staff, only volunteers. Being able to run an organization this big on such a stripped down monetary framework, was practically a miracle. But it was in keeping with the ethic of the job search and in the needs of those we were helping; I didn't want anyone to hesitate to be involved because of the cost. And we still got results.

We've since scaled back our networking events. I'm involved in more things personally with my local neighborhood; my growing commitments to community and with politics have shifted my focus. Networking and finding jobs is no less important but, thank goodness, the economy has improved and now there are an abundance of other organizations. I partner with these organizations, help them with events, and speak regularly to job-seekers. I still view fulfilling these pledges as part of my mission.

When I set out to build the Jewish B2B Network, getting people jobs was just a peripheral focus. However, because of the power of networking, it became a major goal.

Networking is the best way to get a job; it's not what you know, it's who you know. In the job search that's proven. In business, but—let me stress—especially for jobs, you need to be prepared to network. You need to follow up with people who you already know and constantly meet new people. Interact, grow your Rolodex, because every person you meet and stay and touch with is a potential job lead.

Networking functions as a tool that makes you stand out. If people know you, then they are more likely to give you a job, even through a second or third degree connection. For example, college students are often in a very wide pool of candidates for any given position. If they can stand out and connect to someone at a networking event or more casually, the person they connect with may have a contact in a senior level position who can get them to the front of the line.

This same pattern holds true for any age level—it's why our networking events have helped so many people. That said, I always encourage people to meet with me to be specific about who they are looking to meet. If they tell me: "I'm planning to meet Joe Smith at XYZ company because I want to apply to a position at that company," it gives me a greater chance to connect them with the person they really want to meet, or at least be up front about whether I can help them with that immediate goal.

In one organization that I consult for three employees—a receptionist and two people in administrative positions—got their positions solely as a result of my matchmaking. The organization called me and said we need someone to fill our administrative job—but we need them yesterday. I've learned how to ask the right questions from these organizations: the type of computer skills they need, the type of industry skills, and any other strengths they look for in an employee. Then I send them four or five resumes that I have on hand and make clear that it's okay if they don't accept the candidates up front if they lack certain qualities. There are times that I can't find them anyone—especially with specialized positions or with an industry I'm not familiar. But the people that meet me through networking develop a powerful asset because I can relate to companies and know their needs. Meeting people like me—not just connectors to one position but to many positions and industries—is another advantage of networking.

You may also meet people like David Jacobson. David Jacobson owns Chicago Jewish Funerals, one of the foremost funeral homes in the Chicago Jewish Community. David has taught me a lot about what it means to be dedicated to community specifically around jobs.

David gives many people jobs while wearing the networking hat. When people talk to you about employment, they are pouring out their heart out to you; they rely on you to help them. It's a huge responsibility. David is always willing to meet with people and he doesn't just go through the motions—he's always willing to listen and is consistently patient. Every person I've sent him to exuberates about their meeting afterwards; he is inspiring on so many levels. In addition to being my mentor, he's one of my closest friends. I can always turn to him and he can always turn to me. His motto for his business is "The way it should be" and he truly lives by that motto in his interactions with every person he meets. All of his heart is dedicated to the sterling adage "Do onto others what you would want onto yourself." Certainly, meeting someone who's as kind and genuinely invested as David would propel you in the job-search.

We've talked about why networking works, now let's get a more comprehensive inventory of the best advice out there for putting networking in action.

Andrea Storz, Director of Employment Services at the Jewish job center the ARK and the owner of ADMS career counseling, offers more secrets to success with networking. She says that, though there are many steps to networking, reduced to its simplest terms networking is cultivation of relationships. You should start by looking in your own backyard; you have many, many relationships that you may not realize you have. Friends, family, acquaintances, colleagues, even people you barely know—these can all be starting points to establish your foundation for networking.

Dave Ritter, a leader in the world of networking and the creator of the website Network Chicago, joined me on the podcast in 2014. Network Chicago is an online resource that helps professionals find networking events, connections for their business, sales leads, or jobs. It's a central location for all things networking; gathering the disparate networking information spread across the web to make it easier for people to find what the need to become more effective networkers. Using sites like Network

Chicago will familiarize you with a wide range of networking events in your area and will also help you focus on the best events for you.

Another web tool that helps with networking is developing a fantastic LinkedIn profile. I encourage people to create and polish a strong profile even if they aren't looking for a job; it keeps people ready for any opportunity that may come up by ensuring a consistent web presence.

As important as LinkedIn is, Dave says that in growing a business (or finding jobs) making in-person connections is essential. You can find people at events; LinkedIn can be a good method for managing connections—it can't introduce you to people face-to-face! It's better to find networking events through websites like Network Chicago that bridge the gap between online and in-person.

Andrea notes that not every networking event will be for you—it's a trial and error process—though there is no such thing as wasting your time. If you had a conversation with one person at a networking event that otherwise didn't go well, that conversation could still lead to conversations with thirty other people.

You always need a strategic approach before you start through the networking process. "Don't wander through," advises Dave. First, understand your purpose for networking: write down what your objectives and your specific plan for meeting those objectives. It sounds over-analytical, but you can have fun while meeting people and run the risk of not meeting your purpose. Make sure you know your goals and your path so you can guide yourself through the process and actually get what you need to do accomplish.

Andrea agrees: you have to know who you are and what you are networking for. At the same time, you shouldn't put the spotlight on yourself; get to know the other person, understand who you are speaking to, and start a two-way conversation.

In order to capitalize on networking connections, you must be prepared for the next step with a resume. Sheldon Helfgot, president of the Shelright Group, has helped tens of thousands of people with their self-presentation. He helps people tell their stories, from people out of college up to the senior level. He says that everyone needs a resume, but also a bio-sheet, and LinkedIn profile.

Even someone who is gainfully employed needs a resume on hand; you never know when a colleague will let you know about an opportunity and say, "Send me your resume."

Resumes need to be effective both in style and substance in order to tell a good story. Sheldon often sees resumes written in a funnel style: they start wide with general descriptions and narrow to saying "references are available upon request." That's not Sheldon's preferred style. He likes to combine functional and chronological resume formats and he "sets the hooks" with keywords that will tip off a computer reading a resume that you are a good candidate for the position.

People just out of college should only have a one-page resume while someone senior level with greater accumulated experience should have two pages. Most people think that putting duties and responsibilities on a resume will work as an asset; in reality, no recruiter or company hires because of duties and responsibilities. They want accomplishments—"if you can do it for them, you can do it for us."

Interviews, of course, are also a crucial component of the job search. Once you've networked enough to get the interview how do you ace it? Andrea says that the first impression is a lasting impression—you have to prepare for the interview and follow certain guidelines to make a good first impression. Be on time for your interview; don't come too early and definitely don't arrive late. The ideal amount of time to arrive for an interview is about five minutes early. This is so important that it's better to sit in your car than go in; wait until five minutes before. Knowing that your candidate has been sitting outside for a half an hour engenders a negative feeling for the interviewer from the get-go.

Ensure that you present on an appropriate, neat, and together appearance. Be pleasant and friendly; remember interviewers' names and positions—write them down before the interview if you need to.

An interview is supposed to be a conversation with a back-and-forth, but don't ask too many personal questions of your interviewer. If you get too comfortable, you're going to make your interviewer uncomfortable. Keep your questions focused on the position and your strengths in potentially filling that position.

The number of calls that I get from people who have heard of my reputation as a job connector blows me away; I truly never expected it. I spend a lot of my Sundays meeting with people in transition, from all levels of career. I have people who look for entry-level secretarial positions, college kids looking for their first job out of college, CFOs, and people looking for their last job out of retirement. I care about every person that I meet with and I make sure to keep their information on a Google spreadsheet so I don't lose track of them. I send out an email every few weeks to check in with the people I help to see their status on the job hunt.

We've talked about networking, resumes, and interview techniques; however, in order to succeed at a job search you need to know what you want. I got a call from a middle aged woman, Marcy, who had been out of work for several years. She met with me at my go-to Starbucks in Skokie. I sat with her and asked her some questions about what her dream job looked like. It's a question I always ask—I can only get job-seekers in touch with the right people if I know the answer.

She struggled with answering that question. As many times, as I phrased it differently we just couldn't pin down what she wanted in her ideal position. It became clear to me that she didn't have a clear direction for what she wanted her next job to be. It was an alarming realization. I knew that unless she could answer that question to an employer (for an employer that question would be "why do you want to work here?") she would struggle to find a job.

As an initial step to finding this answer, I put her in touch with some of the best Chicago-area social service organizations: the Ark, Jewish Vocational Services (JVS Chicago), and several community colleges and vocational schools. JVS Chicago helped her polish her computer skills, recraft her resume, and professionalizing her image.

In the end, it came down to networking. JVS called me saying they needed my help with networking for Marcy. I'd gotten a call just that day from an employer who said they needed a bookkeeper with Quickbook skills. Marcy was trained and focused—the clarity that she had developed allowed her to answer that crucial question from the employer and say "I want to be a full charge bookkeeper."

She was hired a few days later. Now she's making a living, she can pay her bills, and she can keep her family in the Jewish day school system. It's made her feel amazing to be able to work and to pay forward the help that she got through helping others.

Marcy came back to me after establishing herself at her company. She was asked by her boss to help hire a receptionist. The story had come full circle: she told me that she was now in a position to interview new people though she had been on the other side of the desk just a short while ago. Instead of the person being offered the position, she was now the person offering the position. "You know a lot of people," Marcy said, "Can you send me candidates?" Her story is a testament to the fact that if you follow the guidance in this chapter, you can meet success in your job search. Marcy is an inspiration for me, as I hope she can be for you.

———

I preface every meeting I have with job-seekers by saying I'm not a career counselor and I'm not a recruiter, but I am an expert networker. Every single day companies call me—saying for example "I'm looking for a bookkeeper"— and I can match them with job-seekers on my database. Even though this isn't something I set out to do, over time I've achieved my goal of connecting the dots over and over again. For the four-thousand people in my database currently, I know that I'm responsible for hundreds of people finding employment. There are likely many more people that I've helped find jobs that I don't even hear about.

Making those connections and finding people those jobs are the achievements I'm most proud of in my life in community involvement, and certainly some of the most important commitments in my life as a whole.

FAMILY

Love your family, they'll always be there

BUSINESS COMES AND GOES. We talk a lot about business relationships in this book, but the bottom line is the people who have your back are family. My family taught me about business in particular, but they support me in absolutely everything that I do.

Some days, some weeks, you don't feel so great. A meeting doesn't go as hoped or a colleague isn't nice to you. Whatever craziness happens during the week, you can talk about the mistakes you make with your family and know that they will listen and help you with whatever you need.

I committed to operations for the floats for the Village of Skokie July 4th parade. Every year for this parade I need 25 volunteers and yet, every year, somehow I come up short—I get 18 volunteers. My family has got my back. They're going to be there on July 4th in the steaming hot summer to support me. Because they can call me at two o'clock in the morning and say, "Shalom, I need your help," and I'll help them. That's just what family does.

Business relationships are very defined. You schedule an hour together to manage collaborations, review projects, or refine plans. As per my time management philosophy, I do formally set aside times for dinner dates with my wife during the week; I'll put these on the calendar. However, my weekends are much more relaxed. Then the moments of time we get to spend together are both greater in quantity, and higher in quality, because they aren't limited by the rigid structure of a business meeting.

The time you spend with your family is better not just because you are free of an agenda, but there's also a difference in the way you feel. You can completely and totally let your guard down with family. It's liberating. It's not the way you have to be at work.

I don't put on a show in my business life. I try to be natural, but still, at meetings at Starbucks I behave in a certain business way—I can't help it.

Sometimes my wife jokes that I inadvertently put on my radio voice or a business persona when I'm around her. Of course everyone unconsciously slips in to business mannerisms in their personal lives, but I'm not usually that way when I'm home. On the weekend when I'm sitting at a Shabbat meal, I can kick back, I can be goofy, I can be fun, I don't worry that my family will judge me or think differently of me. There's nothing at stake like there can be at work. We're stuck together, whether we like it or not, and we learn to live with each other as we truly are.

Nevertheless, there are times in any family where you agree or disagree. I grew up in a small family; just my parents, me, and my sister. Since I grew up with them in a smaller house with just the four of us, conflicts would linger. If you have a small family, be aware of this and aim to resolve disagreements quickly. Move on so you can enjoy being around one another and let go of resentment.

Being part of a larger family, getting over conflict is easier. I spend more time with my in-laws now and I've learned with them to let nothing linger. We didn't grow up together, but I don't consider my relationship with them any less tight-knit then with my immediate family. With more people and more relationships, there becomes more space for resolving disagreements.

Business conflicts may dissolve a relationship, but in my family, I have never had a conflict that in any way jeopardized my relationships. I may have an argument with a parent-in-law or a sibling-in-law, but we'll talk it through and we learn to get over it more quickly. We agree to disagree and it's on to the next thing, the next moment of quality time together.

What if your relationship with your family is more complicated— what if you're in a family business? Such a relationship can be difficult; as I've implied, business conflicts can have more teeth than family conflicts. I'd go so far as to say that a family business is one the most wonderful and horrible things out there. Being in a family business is a balancing act and can take some finesse.

I grew up in a family business, doing my dad's invoicing at a very young age, even taking on clients at a young age. I never would have built that experience anywhere else. For a 14-year-old kid, the knowledge and education I was handed proved invaluable.

My dad is a sharp businessman, and my mom got up even earlier than my dad: they taught me my work ethic. I'm able to do so much because I inherited that strong work ethic. When I travel, I have no problem sitting down and working. Even if it's nine at night after being up, I'll still keep working on multiple projects—-that's just what I do. I'm grateful to for growing up in a family business; it gave me one of the major tools that makes me who I am.

Over time, my role increased in our business. I came back from working in New York in 2008. My dad had repeatedly asked me to come into the business and I finally did. When I came in I thought I knew more than I did, especially because I'd worked in the business earlier. My dad saw through this—he taught me all over again, from the ground up.

My dad knows that experience takes time. Once, when I was 16 years old and had just gotten my driver's license, a friend came in from LA to

Chicago. Excited to try out my chops, I asked my dad if I could pick him up. He said no. "You're not ready to drive to the airport quite yet; you have to pick up experience." You need to repeat actions in order to learn them, and with the family business gave me that safe environment to gain experience.

By twenty, I ran the operations of the firm, succeeding because of my father's mentorship. After five years (plus the many years I spent in a non-official capacity), companies and organizations began handing me jobs, and I started getting more involved in my community. Office time started to go down and I felt guilty; I felt I wasn't really running the firm. Finally, I got an opportunity, an opportunity I wanted badly, which would mean stepping away from the family business.

The most difficult conversation I ever had with my father was the moment I told him I was stepping back from our accounting firm. I clearly remember the conversation: I told him that after this certain date I wouldn't be able to take a salary from the firm. I'll always be involved in the firm, I'll always be a partner in the firm, but I'm not going to be in the office anymore. He asked me, "Are you sure this is what you want to do?" He made sure that I wouldn't jeopardize the firm's reputation; that I would retain the title of Vice President. It took months to work out the final details.

Despite being difficult, telling him how I felt was certainly the right decision—it ultimately brought us closer together. These days, I only come into the office to do my taxes, and its allowed my relationship with my parents, my sister and my brother-in-law to flourish. Now we don't talk about business every time we're together. Now we have pure family time.

Family businesses teach people a lot about themselves and train people for work and for life. That's why I consider my time in the family business to be a success, despite having left. I would still do anything for the business.

Though in order for a family business to be a success, you need to achieve that balance. Some families excel at creating a balance; others generate horror stories in which family members don't talk to each other because they've been torn apart by their business.

If you get into a family business, it's important to be clear and to talk through everything so it doesn't damage your relationships. Becky Galvaz, CEO of the Chicago family business Shop4Ties, had to overcome challenges in her family business after the passing of her father. She and her mom worked out roles and responsibilities to come to a solution that satisfied the needs of the business and the sensitivities of the family. Her mom ended up becoming the CFO, doing the back of the house stuff so that Kelly could do the front of the house stuff. "We're at a very good place now," says Becky.

Be clear, not only on how conflict and adversity will be handled, but also on how you'll separate the business and personal. Balance means there needs to be strong lines between business time and family time; this protects both the family and the business.

It's always good advice to leave your work at work and be present when home; this is especially true with family businesses. One guest on my podcast, Kelly Clements, is in the fourth generation of a family business and she says that the question is: what do we talk about at the dinner table? It might always be about business! When a family gets together casually, they should reserve that time to just be together, putting work obligations aside, and concentrating on the personal.

Family businesses require tough conversations like the one that I had with my father, and they require a careful understanding of the difference between business and personal. Having those conversations and developing that understanding is Those worth it. I don't want to see families implode over business; family is more important than business.

Kelly Clements has some great advice on a relationship that becomes the foundation of any family business: the relationship between an entrepreneur and his or her spouse. Kelly is founder and head coach of The EntreprenewHer: The Woman Behind The Successful Man, and has coached entrepreneurs and their spouses for the past 15 years, helping countless couples improve their relationships.

She says, "The spouse is the most valuable asset in any business" — that the real partner behind a business may not be the person on the legal paperwork, but is actually the spouse. In Kelly's first coaching workshop with entrepreneurs and their spouses, she noticed that her clients fell into two camps: those that counted their spouse as their greatest asset and those that didn't. Those that considered their spouse as their greatest asset consistently hit their entrepreneurial goals; growing their business because of the support of their partners.

"It takes two extraordinary people to create one extraordinary relationship," says Kelly. When an entrepreneurial marriage goes wrong, it's usually because the spouse loses his or her identity. Entrepreneurs already struggle to keep an identity when managing the demands of a business. When the spouse loses her identity, both people lean on their relationship to "fill their bucket", ask more from one another than either can handle, and put strain on the relationship. When both people show up complete, fulfilled, and happy to a relationship it builds a supportive foundation and the entrepreneur can truly engage in business free of worry about what happens at home.

Business itself is fleeting. If business goes away, many entrepreneurs begin to have that identity crisis that creates a meltdown and can damage a relationship at home. For this reason, Kelly doesn't encourage that entrepreneurs get their identity solely from their business or from their professional network. When they strengthen their identity in other ways (through a real search for self-understanding) and show up as the best version of themselves in their business, their entire circle thrives. "They become the source that feeds everything around them," Kelly says— leading especially to unshakable entrepreneurial marriages.

The EntreprenewHer includes the word "renew"—a response to the fact that she say many entrepreneurs experiencing burnout in their careers. She loves to travel, to stay busy, and she acknowledges that entrepreneurs wear the grind like a badge of honor. They work 24/7, always plugged in, always available. Such a taxing lifestyle can worsen the most important relationships.

The solution to burnout and the key to healthy entrepreneurial marriages: play. Play is a prerequisite for success. Have hobbies outside of the business and make high-quality free days (as I mentioned I set with my wife) so that you can continue growing together and can take advantage of that time away from work. That way, you'll both rejuvenate and create a high quality of life.

Entrepreneurs and their spouses need to focus on more than just play to stay together. Of all things, "entrepreneurs can be similar to psychopaths"; there are so many opportunities to criticize on both sides of a close relationship. Kelly talks about the compliment to criticism ratio, saying that an entrepreneurial marriage depends on positive affirmations. You need to make sure that you give proper emotional support to your partner because in times of high stress and crisis, it can be easy to assign blame and be hurtful. You can keep your finger on the pulse of the compliment and criticism ratio and avoid tearing each other down.

Financial unity and steadiness also lead to a better spousal relationship, especially in an entrepreneurial marriage. I inherited my money philosophy from my father; he taught me not to spend a penny more than I have. I had a budget when I was in third grade. I certainly didn't have a lot of money back then, but I knew what I had and I knew I could buy anything as long as it was within my means. I still keep track of every dollar that goes in and every dollar that goes out.

My father was raised by his grandmother, in West Rogers Park on Devon and Kedzie. His bubbe would always say, "I don't want any penny that I didn't earn, but I want every penny that I did." Be sure that you pay back others, but when you work hard for your money, also be sure that you get it. Honest in business is honest in life. That honesty comes from taking responsibility for your finances—a joint project when you share your life with someone.

My wife and I were both raised to budget and give ourselves spending allowances. We rented until we could afford to buy a (small) house and pay off our credit card balance every month. Our undergraduate college bills are paid, and I'm up to date with expenses for my Master's Degree program. We use one of our credit cards to earn points for travel to save us money on vacations. These points paid for a hotel, shows in Las Vegas for our honeymoon, and for anniversary trips to places as pricey as New York.

It's not that I don't live life; I just would never travel somewhere or spend on anything that I knew I couldn't afford. I still can support the causes I care about. I give every possible dollar that I can to the charitable organizations I'm involved with, but I allocate that money and don't give it blindly.

Elisheva and I avoid debt by sharing a simple little used car that we've paid off. I need the car for work, so I drive Elisheva to her job. We juggle schedules, save the expense of another car, and insurance and gives ourselves more time together. You'll find that such additional shared time benefits often result from working out finances together.

Live within your means and before you buy something and ask yourself if you really need it. Then get on the same page with your spouse so you can work toward goals together (buying a house and a car were goals my wife and I achieved) and use money in a way that's good for you both.

You and your spouse, you and your family, really want the same thing. You want a loving relationship lasting your whole life. That seems like a lot to ask, but you all were placed together for a reason: to provide happiness and unconditional support to each other.

Still don't believe family always has your back? Look at how my family came through for me:

In December 2010, I'd been running Jewish B2B networking for several months. Jewish B2B had already met with success, positively impacting the lives of many people. I brainstormed: how can I make an even greater impact in the community?

I'd seen a lot of Jewish publications that talked about religion and a lot of business-focused publications, but there was nothing in between. Thinking about the gap between those two groups, I struck on idea to help Jewish B2B and reach out to a Jewish/business oriented audience. I'd publish a magazine called *Jewish Business News*.

I did it all bare bones. I hired a consultant and a freelancer to write articles for it, and a freelancer to edit it. I sold ads that just covered the cost of a printer in Effingham IL, hundreds of miles away from Chicago.

In the freezing winter, my dad helped me load up my small car with 10,000 copies of the magazine in Effingham. We pulled an all-nighter to drive down there, drove back, then got to bed for an hour or two and prepared to distribute the magazines the next night. My sister and mother joined. We looked up every kosher restaurant, every synagogue, every grocery store, every place we could possibly use as a distributor, and came up with an exhaustive list. We made a distribution map with zones for every target neighborhood in Chicagoland.

I recruited every possible family member, as well as a few close neighbor-friends, and started dropping off the magazines in the middle of a blizzard.Only family weathered that blizzard with me all night.

We never did it again. It was not a fun experience.

It was, however, a binding experience. My family knew that doing this was important, they knew it needed to get done, they knew that I was doing the whole thing out of pocket, and that I had to keep costs down. My family was there for me.

Maybe you don't have the best relationship with your family. There could be a complicated history that's difficult to sort out, even over many years. I'm not saying your family relationships will always be easy. But remember that at the end of the day they'll do anything for you, and then you'll see that you can do anything for them. Love your family, live your life.

POLITICS

ENGAGE IN YOUR NATION, UNIFY OUR CITIZENS

BASEBALL. FOOTBALL. DANCE-OFFS. Cooking Competitions. Everybody has that one thing that they follow. They read the stats, they know the names of the players, they even know the names and air-times for the commentators. For me, that one thing is politics.

I followed politics before the patriotic upsurge from *Hamilton*, before you needed a Twitter to really have a handle on the news. Every morning without fail, I jump on the treadmill and watch *Morning Joe*. Throughout the day, I absorb news from a voracious range of online, print, and TV sources: *Chicago Tribune, Wall Street Journal, Crain's, Chicago Business, NY Times, Washington Post*. I'm tuned into my city, my state, my country, my world.

I'm lucky; unlike for some people (sorry cooking show competition lovers) my thing that I follow has a real impact on the lives of real people, whether or not those real people acknowledge this impact. Politics matters, and by following it, I'm part of it.

Many of you may not agree with me. Apathy, even antipathy, toward politics and toward government (the vehicle for politics) is a longstanding American tradition. Thomas Paine, writer of perhaps the seminal text to stoke the American Revolution, *Common Sense* wrote, "Government even in its best state is but a necessary evil." Paine had witnessed the ways in which the government of England, out of touch with the needs of the colonies, had dealt unjustly with the citizens of the nascent America, and questioned the merits of the government itself in his questioning of the status quo. In an ironic turn, the way in which Paine used politics in *Common Sense* (to incite rebellion against the king) eventually defined one side of American politics (inciting rebellion against big government.)

Other criticisms of politics see it as dirty or corrupt. This idea traces back at least to the Middle Ages, with Niccolo Machiavelli writing a treatise on how to rule as a despot in his guide *The Prince*. Some additions follow that advice with another account that Machiavelli wrote about how his prince murdered a political rival. As much as I'd love to believe in play-nice politics, being from Chicago, I know the reality. It's not the fifteenth century, but even a few years ago, a friend of mine who set up political consultant office in Chicago had to pay a "gas meter fee" even if their gas was working perfectly well.

People in power sometimes abuse that power to stay in power, or to get what they want from office, even into the highest rungs of the government. People in power can be out of touch with their base and even be insulated from the requests of those who put them in office by special interests. People in power can only appear to be out of touch, or can be duplicitous, seeming to be in touch when in reality they are hiding their elevated status.

One founder of Greek philosophy certainly had a bone to pick with the politicians in charge. After gaining renown all over Greece for his instruction, at the end of his life, he was persecuted by the government for impiety and died outside of his native land from a stomach virus. This was Aristotle, and it's from his word for city—"polis"—that our own word for politics derives.

Aristotle's examination of politics led him to a radically different conclusion than many modern skeptics of politics espouse. Aristotle wrote in the first chapter of his own work *Politics*, "It is clear that all partnerships aim at some good, and that the partnership that is most authoritative of all and embraces all the others does so particularly, and aims at the most authoritative good of all. This is what is called the city or the political partnership." A political partnership between a government and its citizens exists for the good of all: the purpose of politics is to create common good. Despite the fact that people in government had convicted his own teacher's teacher (Socrates) for crimes he did not commit, and despite the fact that the government would come to pursue him, Aristotle still believed that politics was built to create good.

January 6, 1941: One the worst years in one of the darkest decades in human history. Germany spreads its control over Europe, after already conquering Norway, Denmark, France, Poland, and Yugoslavia. The Holocaust moves with silent efficiency, killing the Jewish inhabitants of each new country Germany conquers. German U-boats terrorize the British Navy, and London is still recovering from the Blitz. A month previous, the United States suffered Pearl Harbor.

Franklin Delano Roosevelt steps up to give the State of the Union. He does not begin by giving weak pretentions that everything is fine, he doesn't cut the ice with a joke or point fingers at people within the administration. He describes the conditions, clearly and without reservation: "I address you...at a moment unprecedented in the history of the Union. I use the word "unprecedented," because at no previous time has American security been as seriously threatened from without as it is today." But Roosevelt offered a solution. He said, "The need of the moment is that our actions and our policy should be devoted primarily–almost exclusively–to meeting this foreign perils"—pledging to overhaul the entire country in support of the war effort.

Roosevelt recognizes the need to act decisively to defend the country because he feels the eyes of history upon him. "In the future days," he says "which we seek to make secure, we look forward to a world founded upon four essential human freedoms: freedom of speech and expression... freedom of every person to worship God in his own way...freedom from want....[and]freedom from fear." Roosevelt recognized that his words in that moment could ensure the future. Ensure the things that people needed in their daily lives to live, things that could be promised to them in a political speech, by a politician, and a giant of history.

The politics of FDR stopped WWII. That's politics as a force for good. He also ended the Depression and made changes to the welfare system that have helped people until this day.

But FDR, despite coming from one of New York's oldest and wealthiest families,graduating from Harvard, and being related to another U.S. president, didn't allow his privileged position to influence how he treated the ones who'd elected him. Though the social norms of his day prevented him from being completely transparent about having a disability, he also didn't allow what others perceived as personal shortcoming to bar him from a life of public office. Roosevelt displayed a zen-like devotion to the idea of politics for good, rising above potential trappings of the self to show the world the true meaning of a public servant.

Ironically, despite being able to put aside hubris in order to lead, Roosevelt developed a cult of personality for many of "Greatest Generation" (the generation that grew up in the Depression and fought World War 2.) Your grandparents, if they lived through that time, may even have a picture of Roosevelt that they kept in a corner much as loyalists in the UK did with King George or Queen Victoria in the nineteenth century. Whole families vote Democrat three generations later because of Roosevelt.

Point being, that even while politics produces those who engage in dirty politics, it also provides the major movers and shapers of history. The secret underlying the difference between the dirty politicians and the people who exemplify politics could be that which gave Roosevelt his strength—his ability to put aside his own position and focus on what the people need.

I experienced something of this sort myself when I visited the White House with a group of small-business advocates a few years ago. We were all very excited to be in Washington, and we decided to check out a local spot for dinner. I keep kosher, and as it turned out there was only one kosher steakhouse—more than a stone's throw away from the meeting we had scheduled for after with the Senate Committee on Small Business. I put my trust in DC Uber drivers and went to the dinner. We had a good time, such a good a time that we lost track of the time. Rushing back in the rain to make our meeting, I was mentally kicking myself, showing up late—what a rookie mistake in Washington D.C.!

We ran up the wet stairs to Mary Landrieu's office; I feared the worst and tumbled in full of apologies. Her attitude threw me completely off-guard; she dismissed anything of our coming late. "How can I help you?" she said. "What can we talk about together?" Mary took our questions, listened to us, and discussed policy with us for hours. She made us feel welcomed and heard—completely counteracting fears that I'd taken up her time.

That's the politics that can continue to do good in the world; the politics where people come down to earth, listen to each other, build relationships, and do good. Clearly, even though some of our clearest examples stand out through the lens of history, many modern politicians are living up the examples of FDR, Lincoln, or Washington, not because they aspire to become those people, but because the things they do reinforce the same political values that those Presidents had.

"We hang on to our values, even if they at times seem tarnished and worn; even if...we have betrayed them more often than we care to remember. What else is there to guide us? Those values are our inheritance, what makes us who we are as a people." Barack Obama writes this in the *The Audacity of Hope*.

In that same book, Obama asks himself our pertinent question: how can a politician become successful without falling prey to the same pitfalls that make them corrupt? Obama talks of his Illinois legislature campaign, saying that he started by talking to people on the street, having conversations with literally anyone who would stop to chat with him. When he becomes senator, he hosts town hall meetings, and connects with those who surprise him—a "flaxen-haired woman from farm country" who adjures him to fight for those suffering in Darfur, an "elderly black gentleman from an inner city neighborhood" who quizzes him on soil conservation. He becomes familiar with their concerns, their hopes, and their dreams. At the end of the meetings, they say to him "Please stay who you are. Please don't disappoint us."

Barack Obama, the first Black president of the United States, winner of the Nobel Peace Prize, was known as "the Great Compromiser." People who worked with him remarked that he had the uncanny ability to bring people from both sides of the aisle together, even politicians hotly opposed on contentious issues. However, saying Obama could "compromise" falls short of his abilities. Compromises get the rep of "everybody loses." People reach an agreement, but they are still muttering under their breath about missing their just desserts.

Now, contrast that with the inauguration of Obama, the consensus that the country reached in 2008. Entire families ran around hours past their bedtime. People danced in the streets. There were even near riots! A never-before-seen atmosphere of hope and optimism permeated the entire race and culminated in Obama's election. By the time that president stood on the podium, everybody wanted Obama.

Obama's capacity to accomplish this nationwide fervor, this raw political enthusiasm, hints at his true ability—someone who reminds people of their values and gets them to promise to commit to those values. While the word compromise means a settlement of difference by mutual concession, the Latin from which it derives, *comprissum*, means a mutual promise. When Obama brings people to an agreement, he eschews the norm and draws on this deeper meaning of compromise. Obama writes, "We have a stake in one another...and what binds us together is greater than what drives us apart, and that if we believe in the truth of the proposition and act on it, then we may not solve every problem but we can get something meaningful done."

I have been a guest in the Obama White House several times and have participated in the White House Community Leaders Briefing Series. It was an opportunity to meet with other community leaders from across the United States and to discuss the direction of community leadership in America.

About the White House: I received an invitation to the White House conversation with the administration on faith-based communities, which I attended. While the meeting was in full swing, I needed to use the restroom. As I walked down the hall to the restroom, my friend Joshua sees me and wants to introduce me someone. As I rounded the corner, I saw Joshua standing by President Obama. Joshua was my primary connection within the White House.

Joshua introduced me as Shalom Klein. President Obama said "Shalom" and gave a handshake that I'll never forget. The handshake was up and down, up and down several times—seeming to last forever. Then President Obama wanted me to make a promise to him. I wasn't too sure about that at first. He countered that it was one of those promises that would be easy to keep.

That promise that President Obama wanted me to keep was to continue helping people find jobs, helping businesses grow, and to come back to the White House. Meeting him was an honor of a lifetime and inspired me to keep my promise to him.

Obama worked his magic on me: the spirit of his method to work peace between opposing parties—helping each party make promises based on personal values that superseded differences which lead to disagreements. Many people still see that he remained true to himself and didn't fall prey to the corrupt forces in Washington because of two other aspects of his politics: his willingness to remember the concerns of those he represented and his simultaneous ability to get them to promise to build something good with him. In the end, even as he became a history-making president, he was still the senator from the Illinois state legislature who talked to the people standing on the sidewalk in his hometown.

Find your values and you will find the politicians you want to follow. Find politicians you want to follow and you will clarify your values. One of the rewards of following politics is that you'll likely find just where you stand on the issues, as I have. I'm a social liberal, a fiscal conservative, and a foreign policy hawk. It took years for me to arrive at these stand-points, even as I might have inherited some of my political leanings from my parents, years of watching the news and reading print sources allowed me to see what I agree with and disagree with. Now that I've solidified my stance, I can begin to see what politicians I support, the models of who I would be like if I, myself, entered politics.

Condoleezza Rice and Mark Kirk—excellent examples of politicians who I admire and whose positions I support; they veer to neither extreme and make sensible policy choices.

Rice worked hard to become a respected academic even before she got to the White House. In her years as a professor, the *Journal of Blacks in Higher Education* rated her as among the top 40 most cited black scholars in the United States. While at Stanford, she became an active leader in her community, joining a group that trained minority students for work and college. She also founded Center for a New Generation, a support fund that gave children in grades three to eight the opportunity to take after school programs in language, computers, math, science, and performing arts. Occasional dignitaries, like Colin Powell, would also visit to inspire the students. Vice President of The Boys and Girls Club of the Peninsula, she said that giving young people a chance to achieve was a way of paying forward the childhood gifts that had led to her own success in adulthood. She continues to support her own artistic and intellectual health; she was famous for playing classical piano at Washington events. Hard-working, well-regarded, caring, self-respecting—these are the qualities I value both in the people I spend time with and the politicians I support.

During one of the most difficult foreign-policy periods in United States History, Condi kept her head. In her time in the Bush Administration, she witnessed 9/11, The War on Terror, The Iraq War, the Lebanon War, Katrina and Bombings in Mumbai among other challenges. Later generations may remember the Bush Administration as one that jumped into the War on Terror. But in Condi's own words, "the days after September 11 were marked by uncertainty and unease that came from operating in dangerous and uncharted territory...We were without a map, but not without a compass. Our guiding principle would be to do everything within our power—and within our laws—to prevent another attack." As a foreign policy hawk and as someone who cares about the security of our country, that's okay with me.

You'll notice that there remains a tone of caution in Condi's words. This measured approach remained a hallmark of her time in office, despite what the spin may say. President George W. Bush once wanted to ad-lib part of a speech on the two-state solution at the UN General Assembly. "Mr. President," Rice once said to Bush, "if you change one comma, you will have changed U.S. policy in the Middle East." Rice brought that measured approach to her work in office even while vigorously defending the rights of the United States and those of citizens of the world. "The United States," she writes, "more than any other country, should understand that the journey from freedom to stable democracy is a long one and that its work is never done."

Sometimes in order to pursue an agenda that you yourself believe in, you must buck party lines. Mark Kirk, through he runs as a Republican, is someone who defends his viewpoints, no matter if it ruffles the feathers on his side. He rescinded his support of Donald Trump as a presidential candidate as the bulk of his party moved in the opposite direction. He believes in climate change, is pro-choice, and supports the Equality Act, which would make sexual orientation considered a category for discrimination under the 1964 Civil Rights Act.

Being willing to leave party lines means that politicians on both sides will often support you. Kirk was ranked as the sixth most bipartisan senator by the Lugar Center and McCourt School of Public Policy, pushing through more bills attracting sponsors from both parties than almost any other senate policymaker. He still remains right-wing on certain military foreign policy issues, like extending nuclear sanctions on Iran. All of these things mean that Mark Kirk is a fighter, but also a collaborator—and I'm betting you know I like that.

Guess what's better than picking to support politicians who are or were already in office? That's right: getting them there. In September 2017, I campaigned for Jennifer Gong-Gershowitz as she ran for Illinois Senate Representative.

Just like Mark Kirk supports job creation and job sustainment in Illinois (his support of the Export-Import Bank was based on its ability to bolster 47,000 jobs in the state), so too does Jennifer Gong-Gershowitz. Pushing not just for job creation but for clean energy, she supports "implementation of the Future Jobs Energy Act to help stimulate job creation with energy efficiency programs." She believes in "expanding credits and incentives for businesses that choose to relocate to or expand in Illinois and create new, good-paying jobs in the state." As I had promised to drive job creation in my promise to Obama, campaigning for Gong-Gershowitz and helping her win on these issues represented a fulfillment of that promise.

Gong-Gershowitz comes from a diverse background and channels that background into insight on her core issues. Jewish and Chinese, her paternal grandparents immigrated in the 1920s, but the Chinese Exclusion Acts almost forced them out. Thanks to a civil rights attorney, her grandparents stayed and her father served in the military and joined the civil rights movement. Jennifer carries on the tradition of fighting for immigrant rights. As a civil rights attorney, she won cases against human child traffickers and perpetrators of forced marriages. Her work to defend immigrants, including Dreamers, led her to politics and to her platform to unite diverse voices with common goals.

I met with Jennifer in person and as soon as I saw that, I respected her and agreed with her values I agreed to work with her. I reached out across my social media network and contacted everyone I could about her campaign. My work culminated in hours of checking websites with instant updates on the votes, hoping that my commitment would pay off.

We won—and against an incumbent.

I don't think everyone is cut out for politics. The long hours, shaking hundreds of hands, giving the same speech again and again in twenty different cities, not seeing family: all these things wear people down and make a stable life more difficult. Politicians on their way to Washington require a level of devotion and commitment that proves they are willing to sacrifice for what they believe in.

Despite this, everyone has a place in politics. Research the issues; make sure you know who you actually want to vote for. Francois Rabelais, the French Enlightenment philosopher, once wrote "Ignorance is the mother of all evils." If you don't do your research, if you don't look to support the politicians you want to support, you are letting the worst of politics replace what could be the best. You are allowing the political system to become corrupted by taking out the need to have you, as a real live citizen, participate.

As Bill Maher puts it:

Freedom isn't free. It shouldn't be a bragging point that 'Oh, I don't get involved in politics,' as if that makes someone cleaner. No, that makes you derelict of duty in a republic. Liars and panderers in government would have a much harder time of it if so many people didn't insist on their right to remain ignorant and blindly agreeable.

I need to be honest and say that right now, I'm worried about the direction the country is heading in. As the left and the right become more polarized, there becomes a dearth of level-headed people in the middle who can keep a clear head and guide the country safely forward. Media and news sources do keep us informed in the new fast-moving climate; however, they increasingly highlight only the voices deemed most notable, the ones to the extreme left and to the extreme right, have become those showcased. These are the most shrill voices, these bring the biggest wow—the "Oh my God, the did they really say that?" But those opinions don't represent the majority of the country. They probably don't represent you and they certainly don't represent me.

In order to stem the divide, more people need to get involved in politics. If everyone at least just learned about the political issues and voted, it would be more than enough.

Sometimes it can be discouraging trying to believe in the efficacy of politics. Even if we manage to stop listening to the extremes on both sides, there's still the fact that our political system is not perfect.

We need to move past this. We have a tremendous opportunity to create good for this country and for the world. Let's prove the good in politics to those people on the edges driving us apart. Thegood of the middle can provide a ground on which all can stand. Let's make politics together.

RELATIONSHIPS

CONNECT, BUILD, AND ENJOY

TRUST, MUTUAL ADMIRATION, respect, follow through. These are the facets that make up enjoyable, healthy, and productive relationships.

I've been fortunate over the past many years to interact with a lot of people. My networking activities put me in front of the crowd, giving me the opportunity to develop relationships with people from every walk of life. I learn something from everyone I interact with. The vast majority of my interactions are positive, far over 90%. There have only been 4 people that, truthfully, I don't want to interact with again—that I had trouble finishing meetings with. That's a very small number for the amount of people I've met.

I travel all over the world and I make connections with people wherever I go. Even when I moved back to Chicago from New York, I stayed in touch with everyone from home. Being able to maintain my relationships drives the success of my personal and business lives. Business and personal relationships keep me accountable in a way that's essential to my own well-being. With almost everyone I've interacted, I've found areas of collaboration and I've seen my business and my personal life expand in uniquely positive ways from the relationships I've built.

You, like most people, should be looking to expand and strengthen the relationships in your life. As someone who's built countless relationships,

I can tell you that there are certain methods to best follow that will guarantee success.

Before I meet somebody, I always put my best effort to find out a little bit about them—even as I maintain an open mind about who they might be and what they might teach me. I put my network to use in the person with mutual colleagues, or I check out their LinkedIn profile. Weeks before, but certainly the morning of, I look at my calendar and I say to myself, "Who am I meeting with today? Am I meeting with this person for the first time or are we getting together again? What would I like to cover in the meeting and what would help me connect with that person on an individual level?" Then I put a concerted effort into making that conversation the best for both parties. I spend time jotting down, either on paper or in my head, things that would be great to talk about with that specific person.

I know that as a result of lack of time, I won't be able to cover everything I want to with a specific person. I so enjoy and I am so committed to building relationships that I have the regret of wishing I could do everything with everybody. If I had more hours in the day I'd meet everyone! Brainstorm charitable projects and ideas and really tap-in to the fact that every person can contribute something to whatever I'm working on. I'm a lifelong learner, and as everyone I meet with teaches me something, I also want that limitless, but personalized knowledge of every person that I can meet with.

The reality is that I can't. You won't be able to either—them's the breaks.

When I think of somebody or I see something reminds me of a specific person, I'll make a mental or physical note to check in. If I have time in the car, I'll call them up right then, or I'll send a text or email to them during the day to see how they're doing and keep our collaboration going.

To preserve any relationship, you need that follow through. When people don't hear from you, they question whether you value the relationship—when they hear from you, it proves you do. The fact that took your time to reach out to them means something!

As you meet continue to meet people and your network expands, you'll see these opportunities to follow up will spontaneously occur. Occasionally, I'll see someone shopping and I'll say, "Wow I haven't seen you in forever!" and you'll keep up the relationship. You'll find that this happens more often and opportunities to follow up will arise naturally, maybe unexpectedly, but in a positive way.

One additional insight: it's easier to stay in touch with people than it is to meet new people. In a networking context, meeting people is work and you'll have an easier time tapping into the ideas and collaborative energy of people you've already met. That isn't to say that you shouldn't meet new people—this is a cornerstone of job and business success that I'll discuss in another chapter. It does mean that you shouldn't let relationships fall by the wayside due to lack of follow through—stay invested in the relationship and it will grow in meaning and mutual benefit.

I enjoy staying in touch with people! I really do! This will happen to you as well the more that you keep up with relationships. It will cease to be something on your checklist and begin to be something you enjoy more and more.

Time management is also a crucial factor in balancing your relationships. If we've made contact for the first time, I remember to put something on my calendar, even if it's for a month out (which happens more nowadays as I get busier.) Being able to stay on top of your professional relationships leads to more time, and better quality time, in your personal relationships.

To go beyond the method and examine the philosophy behind successful relationships, we'll examine the ideas of Steven Covey, whose best-selling book *The Seven Habits of Highly Effective People* has been revolutionizing relationships for decades in the business world.

Covey identifies "Six Paradigms of Human Interaction" that define our relationships: win-lose, lose-win, lose-lose, win, win-win, or no-deal. Win-lose: you prioritize your winning, your pushing your aims, as the first goal in your relationships, even if the other person doesn't get to achieve what they want. Lose-win: you bend over backward for the other person. Lose-lose: you are at each other's throats, aiming (even if not explicitly) to bring mutual failure to the relationship. Win: you just take care of yourself in the relationship, expecting the other person to work their aims out on their own. In win-win, each side seeks the success of the other, and in no-deal, both sides agree that their priorities diverge too much to come together in the relationship and part amicably, and perhaps only temporarily.

According to Covey "The principle of win-win is fundamental to success in all our interactions." Clearly, as much as possible, your ideal vision will be to maximize your win-win relationships and limit your other types of relationship paradigms. Win-win relationships can best be cultivated by those who have strength in character, being able to have the confidence to both be assertive in what they want, and to allow space for the other person to get to their relationship goals as well. Covey says this also requires integrity, maturity, and an abundance mentality—all qualities that you have the potential to develop as you improve your life through this book (and if you read Covey's book).

A win-win mentality is one that can be helped by a high reserve in what Covey calls an Emotional Bank Account: "a metaphor that describes the amount of trust that's been built up in a relationship. It's the feeling of safeness you have with another human being. "Covey details many ways to build up a reserve in this emotional bank account, but the bottom line becomes whether or not you put the investment in to prove to the other person that they should trust you. Trust acts as a catalyst for the desire to achieve a win-win scenario and allows both parties to be more forgiving of the other.

When the reserve is high in your relationships win-wins multiply, but pushing for win-wins (in a respectful way) can also build that reserve. In contrast, pushing for the other types of paradigms results in lost trust and a weakened relationship. You may cultivate negative character traits that will damage yourself and the people that you are around, and will cycle into further non-desirable paradigms. For example, if you consistently engage in win-lose relationships you'll develop aggressiveness. In lose-win you'll develop the tendency to capitulate even if you don't want to. In lose-lose you'll cultivate vindictiveness, and in win you'll foster indifference.

The outlier in these paradigms, no-deal, actually represents a type of win-win and can also reflect character. Sometimes it's better to recognize that a relationship won't work out at that moment than to force a non-win-win situation. This represents an achievement of personal integrity *and* mutual respect as each side truly recognizes the needs of themselves and the other person—just as in a win-win.

However, in order to build the most beneficial win-win relationships, you need good character. Those 4 people I had trouble finishing a meeting with—they didn't have the essential relationship-building character traits that could have made our meetings successful. That became clear to me early on in their meetings. They wanted to be critical, they had an agenda, they didn't want to listen, and they weren't willing to stop talking.

Let me tell you about one of these people. A job seeker, we'll call him Ralph, had gotten a referral from an organization that sends people to me for guidance. Whenever someone reaches out through an organization like this, I hold no reservations or judgements about the job-seeker and I always get back to them right away—this case was no different. I do remember that the scheduling, right off the bat, was a little challenging. Business comes first during the day, so I proposed a Sunday option and evening options.

Ralph countered with scheduling demands: why can't you meet with me at this time? Or at this time? Or at that time? How frustrating, I thought,—trying to make time for someone when I had other legitimate obligations on my schedule. Even so, I found a quiet Tuesday afternoon that I could sit down and meet with him. I said, "I can meet during the day. If that's better for you, I can make it work." We set the time. Though he was mad at me; the back-and-forth took up time and it was two or three weeks past our initial contact. I was getting a bad sense of it even before our introductory meeting took place.

At the first moment of our meeting, I was up at the counter at Starbucks. I said, "Ralph would you like a drink?" He ordered the highest-price item on the menu. It didn't bother me, it was fine, my pleasure. Though I made a mental note.

We sat down and as always my first questions were "What's your dream job?" and "How can I help?" With meetings, my routine is to give myself 50 minutes so that after the meeting I have ten minutes to jot-down follow-up notes. This was still the middle of the workday—calls were coming in and I was still busy. At one point, I looked at my watch— 45 minutes elapsed and he hadn't stopped talking since I asked those first questions! As someone who manages time and values productivity, I almost had a heart attack.

So I stopped him. I asked him, "Have you tried networking? Have you tried putting yourself out there?"

"Let me tell you, you're wrong! Networking doesn't work!" said Ralph.

He spent the next few minutes talking about how I don't understand, how I don't get it. This was after the first 45 minutes of "people are horrible, nobody wants to help," and now "Even you won't give me the time of day"—bringing back up the fact that we hadn't been able to meet after several weeks of trying.

Let me be clear that I never pretend to be perfect. I'm not a career counselor, I'm just there to give my advice and share my connections. There's only so much I can do for anybody, but for Ralph I still made a few more attempts to share my knowledge.

Then he told me if I really wanted to help, I'd personally take him to meetings here, there, and everywhere. It had been an hour and a half of sitting with him, not getting a word in, and only getting criticized.

I said, "I'm going to get up right now, I'm going to give you my card, because that's what I do. I don't think you actually wanted to have a conversation, it sounds like you just wanted to vent about everything that's wrong. As soon as you are ready to form a relationship, to have a dialogue—and I'm more than happy to do that—send me an email."

I walked out of Starbucks. He followed me to my car, ranting. He left nasty messages on my machine when I got home. He ultimately ended up apologizing, as did the organization that sent him to me. Ralph was going through a very tough job search, a very difficult time in his life, and that had driven much of his behavior.

Unfortunately as a result, what Ralph and I created was a not a relationship. It was an opportunity for me to get rebuked for things I wasn't responsible for. Not enjoyable. You never want to raze the foundation before it gets a chance to be built.

I'm not giving this example in such detail to be negative or damage any enthusiasm for setting up meetings and building relationships. This story just gives a perfect "how-not-to" that can act as a guard against you sabotaging your own relationships.

Ralph broke Covey's principles. Instead of setting up an emotional bank account, he'd drawn on my own emotional reserves. Instead of pushing for a win-win, he pushed for a lose-lose.

Ralph also made no efforts to develop the essential qualities of a healthy relationship. He didn't build trust. He didn't respect my time or my efforts. He had no admiration of what I'd accomplished and no appreciation of my ideas. Of course, I couldn't give anything to him; he wouldn't accept what I had to give.

In contrast, I've been able to develop a positive friendship, a fruitful relationship, with State Senator Ram Villivalam. We met in 2011, introduced by a coworker of his, Rebecca, who worked at Jewish United Fund. Rebecca connected us over email and clued us into our mutual interest in small business and suggesting we work on projects together—she knew we had a lot in common from the get-go.

We sat down in a coffee shop, imagining we'd know no-one in common except Rebecca. We started talking back-and-forth about both of our backgrounds and our passions, then getting into the specifics of what we were working on.

He said, "Putting on a small business expo keeps me up at night."

"I've done a lot of those!" I said.

"Oh great," said Ram, "we're gonna have a lot of ways that we can work together."

We brainstormed. Usually in brainstorming, not a lot comes to fruition; in this case, some of the things didn't—as expected. However, the most important things came through. We worked on several small business expos together, one at the College of Lake County, and others throughout Chicagoland. We worked with each other on networking events. We worked together on his race for State Senate. Many more projects and success stories resulted from our collaboration.

It was the first of many conversations. We didn't know a lot about each other but we developed trust.

I knew that when I sent people to him he was going to follow up. People know me and how I interact; I can only send people to those who act in the same way. With him, I knew how he does things. He's on it, like me.

You can see that many of the elements lacking in my interaction with Ralph, elements lacking even in our first meeting, are present in my relationship with Ram. Ram gives me the time to express my thoughts. He shows genuine interest in and admiration for what I do. He pushes for mutual success.

Don't be like Ralph, be like Ram. Be sensitive to cultivating his traits in yourself to foster success in your relationships.

Bear in mind that a lot of business is personal and a lot of personal is business. You associate with people who are like you. I regret that I can't have chemistry with everyone that I work with; I want to find projects that I can work on with everybody! However, it doesn't happen with just anybody. There's always going to be people that you find naturally endearing and can easily create natural ways to work with them. My relationship with Ram worked from the start because we liked each other—we were called together.

That's the initial landscape of relationships, but relationships also take time. I remember growing up and hearing adults saying, "Oh, I've known this person for over a decade." I met such statements with skepticism; it's funny to think that it's true! Now, though, I have people like that. My relationship with Ram took place over the course of many years. It's rare that on the first meeting you find every possible way to work together. Time teaches you everything. As simple as meeting in a Starbucks again and again, as fulfilling as collaborating multiple times together—that's how you build a relationship.

My role models when it comes to relationships: Morrie Elstein, Rabbi Barry Axler, Maureen Dunn. They take professional relationships and make them personal better than anyone I've ever seen, hosting dinner and breakfast parties at each of their homes and developing wide networks of friends and colleagues. I went over to the Axler's for *shakshuka* and they introduced me to several people I found essential to know in an environment that was relaxed and fun.

All three people exemplify how to manage relationships. They've taught me about how business is personal and why, aside for coffee meetings, you should search for opportunities to spend time just enjoying people's company outside of a professional framework. Look for ways to model Morrie, Barry, and Maureen as well. Getting to know people in formal and informal contexts means you'll learn more about each other and like each other more.

Am I proud of my relationships? Yes. Do I wish I could build more them? Yes. Do I find ways to leverage and improve the relationships that I develop? Yes. Relationships are important and your success in relationships will impact every aspect of your personal and business life. Fully acknowledge the other person and, with patience, you'll be able to build trust and experience mutual success. Enjoy building relationships.

COMMUNITY

THE FOUNDATION OF TOGETHERNESS, THE BEGINNING OF PEACE

WHEN I THINK OF COMMUNITY, my Jewish B2B and business card logo come to mind. Two people shaking hands, seeking common ground, finding a connection. Community is a network of relationships: people meeting people. Good ideas are created through this wide ranging coming together, through sharing based on relationships on top of relationships.

Neighborhood is the place you choose and it's your responsibility to get involved in your surroundings with the place that you make your home. You won't have control over who your neighbors are. You'll have to stretch yourself and push yourself out of your comfort zone to build connections with people you may not have that much in common with or organizations you don't know that much about. Likewise, in your neighborhood, there will only be a certain range of activities available or organizations you can join (unless you start something completely new). Even though you have a choice of what you decide to join between these options, they will still be limited by the history of the place you join, which, again, you won't have control over.

On the other hand, with community, you can choose your people, organizations, causes—exactly what you want to be involved with. This level of choice becomes accessible because the world is your oyster: you aren't limited by city blocks to find what you want to find. This can be overwhelming, but it can also be freeing and can be a better way to discover your identity.

Being involved in either neighborhood or community has its pluses or minuses. Some people I know get involved in neighborhood but not in community, some get involved in community and not neighborhood. I personally would never be involved in anything but both. That means that I've gotten involved in the Chicago-Jewish community, the Chicago small business community, but also the Skokie and West Rogers Park neighborhoods. Often these communities and neighborhoods overlap; all the better. Every community, every neighborhood I'm involved in makes me a better citizen, a better volunteer, and a better leader.

The first community that I became involved in, one that helped me establish myself professionally, was the small business community. I realized that much of my identity would be as someone who helps and works with small businesses, and decided to see if there was a community that fit that would help me in developing this aspect of my professional self. I wanted to get to know the key people: who were the influencers in this world of small business in this world of small business in Chicago? I started to answer the who, what, and how of community: who are the people that create each community? What are they are involved in? How can I get involved?

I also prioritized getting involved in the Chicago-Jewish community because of how my parents raised me. I immersed myself in Jewish communal issues: education, Jewish advocacy, and family. I got connected with the organizations in spearheading progress in each of those issues.

As my bandwidth increased, I began moving beyond participant roles to playing leadership roles in organizations such as the special needs focused Jewish non-profit Keshet. This opened me up to a whole different community: the special needs community. I'd leveraged my involvement in one community to the privilege of being involved in another. You will find ways to broaden your range of community involvement if you are open to similar opportunities.

If you care about an issue, you should join the community that backs that issue. You'll be able to be part of the change that the community makes by joining their cause. If you like dogs, join the Humane Society; you'll see dogs being treated better every day. There is no real way that you will be able to take part and take pride in that change unless you take action and join a community. There's no wizard behind the curtain standing there and making the change for you. There's no one else who can do it like you can. There's no one else who can experience it like you can.

As with neighborhood and education, when you join that community, you will find like-minded people that you never otherwise would have had the opportunity to meet. Through your commonality, you will benefit from meeting them just as much as they will benefit from meeting you. I could give you example after example of the people that I've been able to associate with, people that have benefited me professionally and personally, as well as vice-versa, because I got involved in an issue.

One example: I'm chairman of Skokie's Economic Involvement Commission. On my commission, I have the president of a hospital, the senior vice president of a massive national mall management group, as well as other senior professionals. We all meet and work on community issues together, issues that benefit all of us to see progress, because of our personal involvement in the small business community. The longer you stay involved in community, the more you will make these connections with other people and see these connections being made around you.

As mentioned, the danger with finding causes is, the practically limitless range of communal causes: you can get lost. This can be a danger with neighborhood, but it's an even bigger danger with community. Make sure you don't join up with a communal cause unless you are truly invested in that cause. Don't just go with the people who pressure you to join their particular cause, or tell you that you need to be involved in a community. If you don't truly believe in that cause; if you don't really want to be part of that community—forget it. Choose your communal causes with care; otherwise you'll waste everyone's time—including your own—by being unable to commit one-hundred percent. Follow my example: always in all the way, never in the back seat.

Let's say you are coming to a new city and you want to join a community but you don't know where to start. Technology makes things a breeze these days; you can do much of the initial research online. Just as with the job search, the only part of getting involved that should be done behind the computer is the research. After that, you need to roll up your sleeves, get out there, and meet people. Use the internet to research events; don't just research general information about the causes or the organizations. It's a blessing that it's much easier these days to find the information about events than it was before the internet. At the same time, you can get sucked in and forget about having to meet people. Above all, if you are truly passionate about something, your passion itself will fuel you on your search to find the organizations in your chosen community.

People in any community, just as with any neighborhood, will always accept those who want to pitch in to a cause. Find the movers and shapers, and they will let you in. It's a general rule in non-profit that you never want to stay in the same place for too long. A board chair of an organization will be in that position for a few years and then immediately start looking for who is take on the role after them. This works well; in rare occasions, someone will take vicelike hold of a position, but the majority of situations, regular re-appointment is the norm.

This role changing opens space for new, excited volunteers to come in and also creates a culture of upward mobility that you can benefit from when you first join a communal organization. It will quickly allow you to go all in and take a leadership role. Today, you might be checking people in at the registration desk and it may seem like you're not doing much. But it's major; participation is the first step toward leadership.

If you are experiencing pushback in joining any community, don't abandon ship. Find more ways to get involved, find different people, or different avenues for entrance. I'm not of the opinion that there's ever such thing as a lost cause when it comes to joining community; there's always a way in.

As an example, let's say you move to Chicago and are trying to get involved with the Jewish community. You specifically want to get involved with Jewish education, so you make your first step calls to a major Jewish federation with involvement in several Jewish schools in the area. You say that you want to be part of this, to play a role in education in the community as soon as you can. But you aren't getting very far. People don't answer your phone calls or their email replies are slow; they seem reluctant (even though they are probably just busy). Maybe you even get invited to events, but they don't lead to opportunities to make a difference.

There are other ways to get involved. Move from the city level to the neighborhood level, approach specific people at events individually, call a different organization. Try, try again. I've not met very many people at all who have used this strategy and haven't succeeded. Often, initial pushback is a mental strawman and caves quickly once you push back on the pushback. Remember, as I said before, most organizations are eager to have more people; they will accept you once you reach them in the right way.

That's why usually fear or expectation of pushback is typically all that's really in the way with pushback when joining organizations. There's is a huge disparity between the number of people that should be joining organizations and the number that actually joins. It bothers people like me who are involved in many communal causes that we hear and see the same names pop up again and again in relation to similar causes. It's not that it's tiring; it's just a downer when you go from a Tuesday night meeting to a Wednesday night meeting and it's the same group of people. Another night, another cause, but the same cast of characters. We all would really like to see more people involved in our causes.

Part of the reason why it's best for many people to get involved is because the most rewarding process happens when several different strong organizations are able to mobilize their people around a communal cause. This can only happen with a strong volunteer base from all sides, but when it happens, it creates watershed moments in the lives of individuals and their communities.

Through Jewish B2B and my involvement in the small business community, I got connected with an organization called Small Business Advocacy Council. We partnered with the Skokie Chamber of Commerce, The West Ridge Chamber of Commerce, the Small Business Alliance, as well as other invested organizations to lower the cost of filing as an LLC in the state of Illinois.

At the time, according to Elliot Richardson, founder and president of the small business advocacy council, Illinois paid the highest LLC fees in the nation. This took money out of the pocket of small business owners that they could spend on doing things like hiring, buying equipment, paying rent, and supporting their business in other ways. The high fees also perpetuated the perception that Illinois wasn't a good place to operate a small business.

It seemed like getting the fees lowered would be a no-brainer; if the fees were lowered "any loss in revenue to the state would be more than made up by the economic development that comes to Illinois because people would file in this state as opposed to other states," says Elliot. We faced an uphill battle, because even though it had passed through the

Illinois House unanimously the first time, it still had to make it through the senate; we hadn't succeeded in this.

We developed the idea, advocated for it, talked about it at every opportunity, and every council meeting. I mentioned it on my radio show dozens of times saying: "We are trying to lower the cost of filing as an LLC. Join our effort. Here's how." People got fired up. We built up a small army of people willing to fight to change the statute. We succeeded: we got it down from five-hundred dollars to lower than one-hundred and fifty dollars, radically lowering the bar for people who want to start a small business in Illinois.

One person, Dwayne Hirsch, who joined the LLC fight, was starting up a bunch of different commercial entities, and the costs were starting to add up. It got to be very expensive opening up multiple LLCs in his hometown of Chicago.

As a result of our win, he stepped back from opening his LLCs in Delaware and opened them in Illinois. He decided to build his small businesses here; he will hire, invest, and grow clientele where he lives, where he truly wants to be, rather than where he would have been forced to go had we not fought for him and for business owners like him.

Different organizations should talk to each other and work together to help in people's lives. I've frequently seen organizations involved in the same arena, with similar activities and goals partnering to the mutual benefit of all parties and saving money, bandwidth, and time. Anyone in either organization can help organizations to partner. I've personally been able to bring greater efficiency to such partnership with concerted effort and use of my expertise.

When I worked with the Jewish United Federation and Keshet, I put together a matrix of services needed for special needs program, figuring out roles for each organization. We broke up these roles based on personnel and appropriateness of assignment. When we got everyone working in different focused areas, we did a better job; we weren't overlapping and we weren't competing. We were getting done exactly what we needed to get done. Furthermore, we were opening up space and energy to get more accomplished because we weren't wasting energy on overlapping projects. The benefits of pairing far exceeded the effort expended in working out our roles.

Communal organizations should partner over common ground even if it is initially difficult. It's okay if community organizations disagree at first; if one person advocates for one position and another person advocates for the other side. I think that's awesome. Communities need dialogue so that they can be constantly challenging one another. Steel sharpened with steel makes both stronger, though obviously, being on the same page is still the goal. The more people that can add their ideas to the fray, counterintuitively, the more likely it is that someone will have a solution. That's why the strength of multiple organizations partnering can overcome disagreements and bring more resources to the table than just two partners could.

Now that I've been involved in communities for ten years, I can see the fruits of my labor. I see the results of the projects I've talked up a storm for, advocated for, and spent money on—I see these initiatives racing to the finish line. I've witnessed people come in as volunteers and rise up the ranks to become leaders. I've made excellent friends who care about what I care about. All this is true of all of my involvement in jobs, education, neighborhood, small business—but it is especially true of community because everything I do with community encompasses and supports all these areas of my life.

Up until now, I've talked mostly about local community, but I'm always building community; whoever I meet, whatever I create between people, wherever I am in the world. I am a global citizen. As of this writing, I'm about to go to Iraq. Even though it's completely outside the circles I generally move in (outside of my neighborhood, my city, and my country), the interfaith relationships I will build there will create a community between Muslims from there and Jews from here. This community can represent something spectacular: a triumph of togetherness in a history of fractured relationships, a triumph of good over evil. The people who build every community can have just as ambitious goals; communities are tremendously powerful.

The secret to building community is the knowledge that any time you are creating a relationship you are creating goodwill—you are paying it forward. That goodwill circles endlessly between people, going back and forth, and growing stronger. That's why the term community is so broad—community extends to many places. Whenever I travel, I get close to enacting the ultimate goal: to build a worldwide community of peace. Though such a goal may seem pie in the sky, it is a realistic goal as long as we keep relating to each other and sharing the best ideas for change between us.

GET IT DONE

LIVE BY KEY PRINCIPLES, LEAD YOURSELF TO SUCCESS

GIVEN EVERYTHING I'VE JUST SHARED with you, what does it take to get it done? This chapter lays out many of the larger principles I've approached throughout the book. Remember that everything I've told you so far operates around these ideas and you'll be in a good position to follow me and achieve the success I've achieved. So here they are:

Stay goals-oriented. Work Hard. Gain Confidence from Success. Care for Others. Build Momentum. Get Out There. Create Good Relationships.

There's only one way to make it to your goals: you reach them yourself. There is only one person that wakes up everyday thinking about you. Who applauds your successes? Who deals with your challenges? That's just you. Family is a close second, but they'll still never rival you as your own biggest cheerleader and team captain. You are the only person who can get you where you want to be.

I've stayed goal-directed because I don't have a choice. When I complain, nobody listens to me. People might pretend to listen; they might even hear me out for a few minutes. Though they have their own stuff to deal with and they take ownership of their issues as they should. So I take

Get it Done - Live by key principles, lead yourself to success

ownership of my issues and I remain steadfast in resolving those issues and achieving my goals. I remind myself that when I reach my goals, I'm getting the victory.

Working hard is the lynchpin in my efforts to success. I don't do anything half-way. Vocationally, in community, in my education—I don't want to be just one of the people. The people that are remembered aren't the people in the crowd; they're on the stage. It's a big task to get there—it requires everything you have.

That's why I believe in one-hundred percent effort. Half-measures avail you nothing. Would you decide that you are going to half-love one of your family members? Then why would you give half an effort for yourself or anything else you devote yourself to? Instead, give beyond yourself; work harder than you think you can. If you want to accomplish big things, you have to do big things: go big or go home.

Waking up every day with this same focus— I will work hard today— keeps me going. I've been working hard for so long that I don't always think about how hard I'm working during the day. Sometimes at two o'clock in the afternoon, I'm tired and just want to take a break. That's when I re-center and remind myself that I committed to working hard that day and that if I stop what I'm doing, no-one will pick up the slack and I won't achieve what I'd set out to do that day. I fight through. I push forward.

Reaching confidence in success is about picking your battles. I can stay proud of my accomplishments and I can stay confident in my achievements because I'm only involved in projects I'm passionate about. I'm not involved in anything halfway and I can be proud of everything I do achieve and know that I put my all into it.

I'm not good at saying "no", but I just don't have the time to commit to anything on which I can't be a full team player. As tough as it is to say

141

no, I'm not going to put myself in a situation where I can't make a big difference. It's a simple decision for me.

When I am involved, I'm always proud, passionate, vocal, and loud. It's part of how express my enthusiasm for a project. I can't be embarrassed or ashamed of anything I do; it's too much a part of me. The more effort that I put into projects, the more those projects become part of who I am, and the more that my confidence in my successes and in myself grows.

Caring for others allows me to keep things in perspective. As much as I work hard, have a drive to achieve, and remember my individualistic spirit, I remember that I'm not just in it for myself—I want other people to benefit from my efforts. It gives me the inspiration I need to do the things that I do.

I credit my parents with giving me the impetus to care for others. They created a home environment in which everyone was cared for, even members of the community they barely knew. I credit the Jewish values that I managed to glean from my Jewish day school education. In that school system (however dubious the level of instruction), people chip in and people help each other, just like with the model of education. In general, people pay it forward to the teachers, the people that don't make a good living, but do receive a high level of gratitude. I credit my mentors, who offer a constant example of people who do good in many different realms—education, business, community. They have propelled my path and, insofar as there ever is a playbook for doing good for others, they've given that playbook to me.

I was lucky to learn to care for others through these sources in my life because people need a way to develop a moral compass. They need people to point to and say "I'm following their example in how to help others." This goes beyond the instinctual working hard or the logical feeling proud of achievements. Without someone to set that example, people lack backbone. When faced with a situation in which they could care for others, they won't, because they won't know how.

It works from the other side as well: you can be the example by caring for others. Part of the reason I pursue education so vigorously is so that I can set an example and then teach that example better. Just as I grow my investments in myself, I always grow my investments in others, so that my investments can have a larger and larger positive impact on the lives of those I care about.

Working hard is important, but if you want to really get stuff done, you have to build momentum. There's strength in numbers, in making coalitions, in creating organizational partnerships. As you get more people behind you, garner advocates, and build momentum, you will see quicker and greater success. No matter the issue, having a wide base of appeal and having a wide pool of support will always help. Nobody can carry an issue for you, it does take working hard and working on your own, but you can get others to work with you to take things to the next level.

When you get out there, when you network, you can build referral sources, you can get people to your cause, you can get business contacts, you can straight up get jobs.

Referrals are done better in person. The people that want to refer you would prefer to meet you in person; they want some level of trust so that they know they can put you in the right hands.

Networking is a great way to build momentum for your projects and for your cause. For every person you already know who wants to be a part of your cause, there are ten people you don't know that might also want to join. You'll never meet those people unless you get out there, but if you do, you'll be surprised by the fact that you can find passionate people, or people willing to pitch in and participate.

Businesses thrive by building wider networks. It means more customers, more clients, more potential business partners, and even potential buyers further down the road. If a business isn't expanding, it runs the risk of going stagnant and then failing. Getting out there and meeting people is a sure-fire way to keep your business healthy.

Everyone is always looking for a job to some degree and networking is like the real life LinkedIn. But it's better than LinkedIn! It's a more seamless platform, messages have unlimited characters, and you don't have to worry that you don't look good in photographs. You can socialize and build comfort without being stuck in your room. People will often feel that they've really gotten to know you, so they'll be more willing to give you a job opportunity than if they just saw your resume online.

As I've said over and over again, networking works. You don't know how meeting people will pay off and you don't know who will end up being that major connection that you'll need for your job, or your business, or your cause. You need to get out there and meet people if you want to get to that person.

If you just get one thing from my book, get that you need to create and nurture relationships. You need to work harder, not smarter. As hard as you can work as an individual, you will never be able to work as hard as you could as a team. Surround yourself with good people and never ever take people for granted. Genuinely try to help people. If you build real relationships you'll enjoy your day-to-day life more, and you'll do good.

One last note: you may have noticed that the goal of this book is not to make you personally wealthier, or cooler, or more popular. It's not harder, better, faster, stronger. The goal of life is not to be the sole winner; it's to help people win together. I hope that by reading this book, I've developed a positive relationship with you, you've developed a better relationship with yourself, and you've grown in your relationships with others.

I live what I preach. I'm not using this book as a get-rich-quick scheme. My goal in life is not to enrich myself. It's to better the communities I work with and try to make the world at large a better place. I live it every single day, some days better than others, in a way that is way beyond vocation. Vocation is just one part of my life, and recognizing that allows me to stay devoted to my overall mission and stay in line with who I am. That's why I can say today that if I could do anything in the world, it would be what I'm doing right now. I have found a way not to sacrifice parts of myself so that I can live. I've expanded what I'm doing beyond what I need to be doing and into what I want to be doing. That's how I make myself into a person, not just a cog.

Many people can feel trapped by their jobs, by their families, by any number of life situations. Break through this feeling by concentrating holistically on other elements of your life and by concentrating on the people in your life. Work in multiple arenas, develop relationships with mentors and peers, and you'll be able to become more invested in yourself. You'll find out exactly what you want to be doing and then you'll be able to say the exact same thing that I can say to you today: I am the person I want to be, doing what I want to do.

You'll never be able to do this process without having the right intentions; unless you want to help others in addition to yourself. You'll always end up sacrificing important pieces of yourself in pursuit of cheap personal fulfillment.

I believe in you and I believe in the people around you. With this book, with a good head on your shoulders, and good intentions in your heart, you will become the business person, the networker, the community organizer you've always wanted to be. You will get down to business. You will get it done.